A YEAR AT THE LEMONDROP

A YEAR AT THE LEMONDROP

How one family bought
a house,
started a short-term rental,
and lived to tell the tale

All during a global pandemic

Zephyrus White

Paula Vandenberg White

Blue Feather Books

Copyright © 2024 by Zephyrus White

All rights reserved. No part of this book may be reproduced in any manner whatsoever without written permission except in the case of brief quotations embodied in critical articles and reviews.

First Printing, 2024

"IT IS NEVER TOO LATE TO BE
WHAT YOU MIGHT HAVE BEEN."
~ GEORGE ELIOT

CONTENTS

	Forward	1
1	You've Got to do Something	3
2	Covid Hits the World and Me	7
3	Don't Fall in Love	9
4	Do We Pull the Trigger?	18
5	How Do We Choose?	23
6	What's Inside	29
7	The Window Is Closing	33
8	Funding	41
9	Numbers	43
10	What's in a Name?	49

CONTENTS

11 | There's No Escape. Or Is There? 55

12 | Paula's Story 59

13 | We're Live 79

14 | What Does the House Need? 93

15 | My Trip to the Lemondrop 100

16 | Happy Thanksgiving 110

17 | How Are People Going to Know That You Exist? 119

18 | Our First Turnover 129

19 | How Long Is a Day? 140

20 | First, Do No Harm 152

21 | It's Snow Globe Time 161

22 | Approaching a Cliff 168

23 | Plumping Up Our Listing 175

24 | Iceberg 182

25 | Mud Season 190

CONTENTS

26 | Promote 195

27 | Bon Appetit 200

28 | Smooth Sailing? 204

29 | You Can't Please Everyone, Even When You Do 212

30 | Alexander's Trip to the Lemondrop 222

31 | Fall 228

32 | We Made It Through Our First Year 234

ACKNOWLEDGMENTS 243

Forward

This is a story. It's my story. It's the story of how my family and I opened a hospitality business smack dab in the middle of a global pandemic. It's the story of our first year's journey with the Lemondrop Lodge.

This is a memoir. It's also a how-to book. In the decade and a half since Airbnb burst onto the scene the popularity of short-term rentals has exploded and along with it a whole new sector of the hospitality business. Since 2007 when Airbnb launched with one listing it has grown to over seven million listings. Along with this burgeoning new industry have sprung countless gurus and experts with promises of passive income and easy money. That's not what this book is about.

This is the story of my family's adventure; our leap into the world of short-term rentals. It is an honest account of our successes and our failures. Our journey from dream to reality. I will share what we've learned along the way. I will show you our mistakes so you don't have to repeat them and give you a realistic view of what awaits if you choose to make your own leap into the world of short-term rentals.

I hope that you will find our journey through the first year's perils and pitfalls entertaining and perhaps even inspiring. The opinions and advice in this book are mine and provided as-is and as such do not reflect the opinion of Airbnb, Vrbo, or any other short-term rental platform.

1

You've Got to do Something

You've got to do something. I lay on my apartment floor, staring at the ceiling and twirling my finger around a thread in my brown shag carpet. It's 2020, and we are six months into a global pandemic.

My name is Zephyrus, and I am many things. I've been a dancer, a carpenter, a rock climber, even a giant strawberry; the list is as long as it is bizarre. Most recently, I worked as a specialty performer with the Metropolitan Opera in New York City. If you go to the opera and you see someone on stage and they're not singing, but maybe they're sword fighting or maybe they're juggling, or maybe they're falling down some stairs, there's a pretty good chance that someone is me. More than twenty years ago, I packed up two suitcases (you were still allowed two free checked bags on an airplane back then), and clutching a one-way ticket, left a little town in Kansas for New York City.

As a boy, I'd always known life would take me out of that little town, but I didn't have an inkling just how far life would take me. That life led me on many twists and turns and many adventures, but it seemed to have left me here on the floor in my little apartment with one thought echoing in my head: *You've got to do something.*

Six months ago, I felt overwhelmed. I had an amazing job: a dream job. I made my living as a performer at one of the most prestigious performance companies in the world. I wasn't famous. I wasn't rich, but I was one of those most rare of creatures— a working actor. I'd spent years struggling, hopping from one little regional job to another, to a tour, to a short run of some obscure show in the city. It was hard, it was all-consuming, it was beautiful. It was everything I'd dreamt of in that little town back in Kansas. But, if we're lucky in life we evolve. I had evolved.

The job at the Metropolitan Opera had come along at the perfect time in my life. I was burnt out. I wanted something different out of life, but I didn't know what. The life of a working actor leaves little time to explore anything else. When you're not working on a show, you're working on getting your next show, keeping your skills sharp with unending classes, and constant auditions. Like I said, it was a beautiful life, but I was beginning to want something else. I liked learning new things and I always operated under the assumption that the more random things I could do, the more opportunities there would be. It probably started in Kansas. There's not a lot to do besides learn silly skills and daydream. Who would have known that my collection of random skills would land me a plum job at some place like the Metropolitan Opera? At this point in our story, I'd been fulltime at the opera for ten years and ten years is a long time even for a plum job.

I had many ideas of what I might do— where I wanted to take my life.

I'd earned my sailing license. See, I thought I'd buy a boat, build a sound studio on board, and then sail the world living cheaply and making my living as a voice actor. (Yes, I'm also a voice actor.) That seemed like an amazing life, to experience what the world has to offer. Live life free! I was pretty serious about this idea until I realized that when you own a boat you are quite literally anchored to it. It is maybe the least free life out there.

I wanted to open a little bookstore/bar. A place with a little stage in the back— books and coffee by day and a bar and local talent by night. I still want to do that, but back in 2020, the chasm between where I was and pulling something like that off loomed wide.

I had a lot of other ideas. One of them was to buy a property and rent it out. But not just a regular residential rental. With a traditional rental property, you're stuck with a tenant and all the headaches that can involve. I wanted to do a short-term rental: a vacation property. I would use the income to pay the mortgage. I would build equity in the house. But most importantly, I would own a home. You see, as much as I dreamed of freedom, I also longed for a home. My life in New York had been a string of apartments that always felt like someplace that was okay to crash for a while, but never like a home. Not only that, my grandpa's words still echoed in my head:

"There's only so much land," he'd say. "It's a finite commodity. You gotta own some land. That's what you gotta do."

I'd spent the prior four years looking at houses and dreaming.

Now I was furloughed from the Met, trapped in my little apartment in a city being rent by the plague.

2

Covid Hits the World and Me

Covid hit New York City hard. At the beginning of March 2020, we started hearing about a new virus. Like most people, I didn't think much about it. I assumed it would just blow over quickly. By the end of the first week of March, the virus was spreading fast and there were rumors that the Met might have to shut down for a few days. I still wasn't concerned.

The morning of March 12th I went climbing at my gym in the morning before rehearsal. When I finished climbing and retrieved my phone from my locker a message awaited. *Rehearsal is canceled.* It's funny to say this now, but my first reaction was a rush of joy. I'd have a little bit of time to myself. Between rehearsals and shows, I had started feeling like I was trapped- like the Met owned me. There was a life outside of the theater that I wanted to live. Not only that, it's a horrible feeling, feeling owned. A couple of days off would be wonderful.

The next day the Met canceled two weeks of rehearsals and performances. I was still excited. I could use this time to recalibrate and maybe start to make some real designs on a new life. By the end of that first week, everything changed. The Met furloughed all employees and canceled the rest of the season. Restaurants, bars, gyms— they all closed. The shelves in the grocery store were ravaged. Leaving the apartment meant masking up, gloves, and a complete scrub down when one returned home. The streets of New York City were eerily empty. I'd heard that a field hospital had been set up in Central Park and meat storage lockers were being used for bodies. I lived a few blocks from a hospital. The sirens never stopped; ambulances constantly going to-and-fro. It set my nerves on fire. Then one day, they turned the sirens off. The ambulances still rushed the unlucky to care without pause, but they were the only ones on the roads. That silence was worse.

The world had shut down. The virus was hitting every corner of the globe and people were dying by the thousands— daily. It was too much for me. No one knew what to do, how to fight it, how it spread. There was nothing to be done. I holed up in my apartment, and the weeks turned to months.

This is the world in which our story takes place.

3

Don't Fall in Love

"Don't fall in love with it!"

It is August 2020. The Covid-19 pandemic is in full swing. The world has locked down, and as much as Vermont can feel like Shangri-la, Vermont is in fact part of the world, and it is locked down tight. No one is allowed to enter the state. Only the most essential of businesses are allowed to operate. You're not even allowed to gather in a private home with family members from another household.

It was into this environment that Poppy (the bright orange Prius) and her crew of burgeoning entrepreneurs breached as they crossed the New York-Vermont border.

Not to throw shade on New York— I've lived in New York for the majority of my adult life— but you can tell when you cross the New York-Vermont border with your eyes closed.

You're bouncing along on a washboard road and then all of a sudden, the road smooths, birds start to sing, and you can feel a warm glow fill your heart. The second two might just be me, but Vermont road maintenance is second to none.

To be honest, we were all afraid there would be State Police at the border stopping people to check their residency status. It may seem a little silly now, but back in 2020 the world had descended into something out of a dystopian novel, and one really didn't know what to expect. The little Prius carried three of us on that day's adventure: me, my brother Xanthus, and our mother, Paula. The Prius was Paula's and she'd named it Poppy.

We had all quarantined. This was back when you couldn't find Covid tests anywhere, but the quarantine gave us some confidence that we weren't carriers of the world's current nemesis. We'd packed our food so we wouldn't need to stop at a restaurant. When it was time for gas, Xanthus masked and gloved up and paid at the pump. Just between you and me, I still felt guilty. Vermont had the lowest Covid case count in the country, and I felt that should be respected.

However, we were on a mission. Thanks to Zillow and Redfin, we'd virtually perused every property within a fifteen-mile radius of Mount Snow. Not only that, we'd connected with Vermont real estate broker extraordinaire, Adam. Adam was invaluable. He knew the area and he knew the market. He'd helped us narrow our search to a stretch of road about five miles long running right next to Mount Snow.

"Anyone who wants to ski is gonna want to be on this road." That had been his advice.

Seemed reasonable. At least that's where we were going to start. Our options for action were limited and I think all of us burned with a desire for action; especially, after weeks of lockdown with no end in sight. It was worth the three-and-a-half-hour drive each way just to have a look at the outside of some of these properties. Paula was armed with a stack of printed listings. I was armed with a notebook full of virtually illegible notes. And Xanthus was armed with the willingness to drive seven hours round trip as well as all over West Dover.

The first on our list— Kingswood. I remembered seeing one of the Kingswood yellow houses listed several years back while traveling through Vermont with a friend of mine. This brings me to an important point. When you're looking for a property it's pure gold if that property is unique and memorable. If you already own a property, and it isn't particularly memorable, you need to find a way to make it unique. Find a way to make it the kind of place that will stick in someone's mind. There will be hundreds of listings on the big short-term rental sites and when people are scrolling through you need something to grab their attention. This means a unique hero picture. It doesn't have to be a full shot of the house. It can be an amazing bedroom, a beautiful view from a deck, or a spectacular welcome basket. Whatever it is you need something that will grab a potential guest's attention and lodge in their memory.

I'd scrolled through hundreds of property listings over the past few years, but the little yellow house that looked like a fairytale castle was curled up cozily in my memory from nearly half a decade ago.

Back to our story. We turned into the Kingswood property. Kingswood is one of about ten little communities along this road. From the moment we turned into Kingswood, we felt a tingle of magic. The road snaked down the side of the mountain. Across the valley, in which lay West Dover, you could see another mountain rising into the sky. All of the houses were yellow and all of them the same design. Usually, this sort of thing would be abhorrent to me, but this was different. Each house sat on a different angle and perched onto the mountain in a different way. And the landscaping... The landscaping managed to be both wild and meticulously designed at the same time. I know I said it was magical before, but that's really how it felt. It felt like we were entering some elven village from a book.

I could see my brother's and mother's eyes widen with wonder.

"Don't fall in love with it!" I said. "This is the first place and there's bound to be some catch."

Our list contained four Kingswood properties for sale. Paula's printed-out listings included some pictures and a brief description, but I was sure there was a catch. Maybe this was a private community and we'd never pass the application process. Maybe it was a retirement community and we wouldn't qualify. Maybe it was simply a bait and switch and the properties were way more expensive than listed.

"Don't fall in love with it," I reiterated.

Each Kingswood listing was slightly different. A little different square footage. A little different price. Different orientation on the mountain. The first was the smallest of the four, but its orientation put the entrance behind the road facing the woods making it feel very private. So private, in fact, that Xanthus and I went into the woods behind to relieve ourselves. I'll remind you that we were in a pandemic and there would be no stops for bathroom breaks.

The next house was equally beautiful and the one after that and the one after that, but there's not a lot you can do when you can only look at the outside. We were also a little afraid someone would ask what we were doing there, but Kingswood was pretty much deserted. Apparently, most of these homes were vacation homes meant for skiing and it was August. I suggested we move on. I could tell Paula and Xanthus were already in love and I was desperately fighting to keep these yellow houses out of my own heart as well. I wanted to get moving.

Next, right across the main road— Bears Crossing. These properties were about 30 percent less expensive than Kingswood and had a completely different feel. The Bears Crossing properties were much more rustic. Inside, according to the pictures, lots of wood panels and a real ski lodge feel. Well, when I say a real ski lodge feel, I'm talking about a reasonably priced ski lodge from the 1970s. The Bears Crossing units were not without charm. In fact, they were very charming, but sans the magic of Kingswood. These were also mostly two bedrooms as opposed to the Kingswood three.

This is something into which we'll go into more detail later. You're going to want to put some thought and research into the number of bedrooms. There is definitely a point of diminishing returns. The number of bedrooms will also play a huge role in the types of guests you both target and get. We'll talk more about choosing the types of guests to target as well. Now, back to Bears Crossing.

Bears Crossing has a nice outdoor swimming pool, but of course, in Vermont, that's only going to be an asset a few months out of the year. It also has tennis and basketball courts. Here's another thing to think about when choosing a location and property. Is your draw seasonal? A seasonal draw can be a powerful thing, like a beach house or a ski lodge. If you are going the seasonal route though it's certainly an asset to have something to offer that will appeal to guests off-season. We kept Bears Crossing on the list. These units were by far the least expensive, and we didn't know what we could afford yet.

Next up, Timber Creek. There was only one unit for sale in Timber Creek. It was gorgeous, sleek, and modern. But I've been remiss. Before we get to Timber Creek, let me introduce you to our whole team. I say team, but we're also a family… literally. At the time, we represented ages from twenty-eight to seventy-three. We had a former ballet dancer, two mothers, a grandmother, someone who grew up in South America and was educated in Europe, someone with more than two decades of experience in some of the best restaurants in New York City, and a regional manager of one of the largest banks in the country. This was our team. This is my family.

All of this diversity of experience gave us one of our greatest strengths; our diversity of viewpoints. Our team included me, Paula (my mother), Xanthus (my younger brother) Anemone (my sister), and Francisco (my brother-in-law).

A fancy bathroom wouldn't even have made my list of things to consider. As long as the place had a bathroom that looked functional, that'd be fine by me. But for Anemone, a fancy bathroom was among her top three desires. That's one of the first things she looks for when browsing a short-term rental listing. If you don't have a team with a wide range of viewpoints, you're going to want to enlist your friends or colleagues. It's important to remember that you're not picking your dream home. You're picking a place to fulfill other people's dreams.

Of course, we couldn't see the inside of Timber Creek. All we had to go on there were the pictures, which looked very nice. We could see into the clubhouse a little. It had a large pool and a hot tub. It was very fancy, very nice. It was also quite a ways from the unit so one would have to drive if they wanted to go for a swim. Paula, Xanthus, and I weren't impressed with the outside of the Timber Creek place. It looked like any apartment complex you could find anywhere in the United States and while it was in the midst of Vermont gorgeousness, the unit itself was only surrounded by a parking lot. There was a deck, but you'd have to look over a lot full of cars and concrete to enjoy the nature.

We looked at a couple of other units in different complexes that, for one reason or another, we quickly knocked off the list. The day was starting to fade, and so were we. Plus, we still had a three-and-a-half-hour drive home. Before we left, however, the three of us did want to have another look at Kingswood.

"Don't fall in love with it!" I said again as Poppy the Prius carried us through the Kingswood community.

A winding stream wove through the trees, around the houses, and down the hill to a trailhead. We followed that bubbling brook and parked. The map promised a little pond and we all needed to stretch our legs before the long drive home.

As we exited Poppy, we experienced a palpable sense of peace. It's hard to describe. It wasn't so much that it was quiet, although it was quiet. It wasn't that there wasn't any hustle and bustle. There was just a profound sense of peace in the air. We didn't speak much. I don't think any of us wanted to break the spell. Walking around, it felt like being in a cathedral. We walked down a couple of trails but failed to find the promised pond.

I wanted to live there. Tension that I didn't realize I was holding evaporated and my shoulders dropped. Each breath filled my lungs with pure air that sent oxygen racing through my veins to fill my heart with a warm sense of well-being.

Don't fall in love with it! This time the words were inside my head and just for me.

After our legs were stretched and our chests were tingling with possibilities we hopped back into Poppy and started the drive home.

4

Do We Pull the Trigger?

We made it back to New Jersey without incident and bubbling with excitement. The three of us briefed the family on all we'd gleaned from a drive through the properties. We put the listings up on Anemone and Francisco's big-screen TV. Anything that wasn't on the road running parallel to Mount Snow was out. Bears Crossing was the most affordable and certainly wasn't without charm, but we crossed the Crossing off the list. We wanted to go a little higher end if we could. It's very important to think about the guests that you will be targeting. Skiing is expensive. We're right next to a mountain. We wanted to pull people who had a little extra money to spend.

That left us with the four properties in Kingswood and the one in Timber Creek. Xanthus, Paula, and I were partial to the Kingswood properties, having experienced them ourselves. Anemone and Francisco were drawn to Timber Creek.

Most of these little mountainside communities had a sports center with a little gym, pool, etc. Kingswood and Timber Creek were no exceptions.

Timber Creek was definitely high-end— freshly renovated with granite countertops and a jacuzzi bathtub in the master bathroom. It's important to remember when buying, or even just decorating your short-term rental, that you're doing it for your guests. It doesn't really matter what you like. You want to attract your target audience. I've always been an outlier. That's why I didn't want to rely solely on my own instincts. Just because I was enamored with the magical yellow houses didn't mean that others would be so stricken. Anemone and Francisco are much more mainstream. They are also more solidly in our financial target audience. The Timber Creek property had something else going for it, or so we thought. The listing said that it came furnished.

You can't just rent out an empty house. Not only that, you want it to feel like a home and that takes more than the bare essentials. Furnishing a house would be expensive, and the fact that this one came furnished was a huge bonus.

So I acquiesced. I was so excited about the prospect of starting this business that I didn't much care which property. I just wanted it to be successful.

I'd thought about this moment for three, maybe five, years. I would have probably weighed the pros and cons for another four or five years, but Anemone and Xanthus are much more jump-iners. It's great if you can put together a team that balances caution and planning with action. We were lucky in that respect. The next morning, we put in an offer on the freshly renovated Timber Creek property.

I'd expected a colossal panic to set in. This was by far the most money I'd spent on anything in my life. It would take a significant amount of the savings I'd scraped together and earmarked for creating a new life.

Beyond that, what did I know about running a short-term rental? And for Pete's sake, we were smack dab in the middle of a global pandemic that had no end in sight.

The panic didn't come. I sat alone in my apartment, and I felt good. All day. It felt real. It didn't feel overwhelming, just exhilarating. I basked in that exhilaration all morning, into the afternoon, until the call.

My phone buzzed. It was Anemone. It was bad news. The property had another offer. I masked up, put a spare set of clothes in my backpack, and headed for the bus.

This was the protocol in those days. If I had to take the bus out to my sister's, I would wear gloves and a mask. As soon as I got to their house, I would strip down in the backyard, put my clothes in a plastic bag, scrub my hands, put on a fresh set of clothing, and only then enter the house.

We had a family meeting. How badly did we want the Timber Creek property? Pretty badly it turned out. We raised our bid by $20,000. I'm not sure what we were thinking (other than we really wanted the place).

This can be a big pitfall. I'd already been picturing the condo as mine and now it felt like losing something that was already mine. The psychologists call this loss aversion. That extra $20,000 was too much. We shouldn't have raised our offer. It didn't matter, though. By evening, we'd lost the place. The other bidder made a cash offer that we just couldn't match. It was disappointing. It was also a stroke of luck.

So now we were down to the Kingswood properties. There were four of them, all slightly different. One a little cheaper, but also 350 square feet smaller. One with a hot tub. One with a cool embedded wine refrigerator. We put the listings and pictures up on Francisco's sixty-inch TV and debated into the evening. Each of us had opinions and reasons, but in the end, we decided any of the four would be wonderful. How then to decide on which one to put an offer? We were now much more pessimistic about our offer being accepted. I think we all wanted to remain a little aloof and not get too attached to any one of the places.

When you list a property as a short-term rental, you're essentially selling an experience. If you're just offering a place to crash, you're never going to thrive in the short-term rental business. What does your place feel like? What do you want people to feel when they stay there? What kind of people are you going to be targeting? All of these are important questions. You need to come up with a cohesive compelling brand. Because that's really what you're doing. You're building a brand.

We had an idea of who we wanted to be targeting. Financially, we wanted the middle/upper-middle class. We didn't want to target the budget traveler because, well, we wanted to charge enough to cover our mortgage and make a profit.

We'd chosen a ski location because the mountain would be a draw, but also because skiing is expensive. The people who ski generally have money. So why not target the rich? First off, we couldn't afford a place that would appeal to the very rich. Even more than that, though, Xanthus's and Anemone's experience in the New York City fine dining industry had taught them that along with money comes expectations. Often, the rich have overly inflated ideas of what they deserve. They are rarely delightfully surprised by something, but are much more likely to be annoyed at some detail that didn't meet their expectations. We didn't want that in our lives.

What to do now? There were four options and they all were in Kingswood.

5

How Do We Choose?

Time for another family meeting. If this crazy idea was going to happen it was going to happen in Kingswood. After we made the offer, I'd become very excited about the Timber Creek property with all its posh glamor, but now that we were back looking at yellow houses... I don't know. I don't believe in fate, and I don't buy into intuition. I do, however, believe that when you've put in enough hours and gathered enough data it all integrates and simmers in your mind and can give you what feels like intuition or fate. I was feeling that now.

As I mentioned before, I'd been browsing Zillow dreaming of real estate for nigh on half a decade. I'd seen hundreds, nay thousands, of listings and when you look at that many houses they blur together. Still, I remembered the little yellow house that looked like a castle. I had let myself diminish the importance of this when we put in the offer on Timber Creek. That was a mistake. Luckily, fortune had given me a second chance.

You may not be so lucky so take this point to heart: If you're buying a property to launch your short-term rental business, heed the listing that keeps popping back into your head. When your potential guests are scrolling through Airbnb or Vrbo they're going to be overwhelmed too. They may look at hundreds of properties before choosing. They may just be browsing for some time in the future. You need a place that's going to lodge deep in their brain and whisper, *remember me? Aren't I special?*

Kingswood with its unique architecture and beautiful landscaping design was that. It may not be every guest's cup of tea, but it was sure to be memorable.

At that time in 2020, the real estate market was on fire. Prices were just starting their spectacular climb and in southern Vermont, owners were looking to cash in on their vacation homes. We had the choice of four little yellow houses in Kingswood.

Choice A was the least expensive: about $20,000 less than the most expensive. It was also the smallest at 1,850 square feet. The layout of all of the houses seemed very similar, but the brilliance of the Kingswood layout was in the positioning and the landscape. They all looked like they fit together, but they all looked unique and special. Choice A was situated with the entrance toward the back which gave it a very private feel. It was also the closest to the clubhouse.

Choice B lay a few houses down the mountain. It was $10,000 more than Choice A, but also boasted 2,150 square feet.

Choice C lay even farther down the mountain. It was probably far enough that people would want to drive up to the clubhouse, but this one had a hot tub on the deck. A hot tub for a vacation home in a ski town seemed almost essential. This one was also 2,150 square feet and the most expensive at another $10,000 above Choice B.

Choice D was around the corner in a little cul-de-sac. It was probably the least private, sharing the circle drive with two other houses. It was a little smaller than B and C but larger than A. This one was the second least expensive: $5,000 less than B and $15,000 less than C. However, its defining feature was inside. The kitchen was furnished with stainless steel appliances which looked particularly cool. Not only that, but all of these houses had a little quirk. The kitchen, living room, and dining room were an open floor plan with beautifully vaulted ceilings. An island counter divided the kitchen, with one end facing the living room. A, B, and C all had a little TV embedded in the end of the counter. It looked silly in the listing pictures. Why would you put a TV there? House D had a wine fridge in the end of the counter. That looked cool.

We gathered together, put the listing photos up on Francisco's TV, and started the debate. Xanthus and Paula liked Choice A because of the privacy. Anemone thought a hot tub was super important and so was partial to Choice C. I liked the wine fridge and stainless-steel appliances which left me leaning toward Choice D.

We all had different preferences, but they weren't strong leanings. There wasn't going to be an argument over the choice. If anything, the properties were equal enough in all of our eyes that the difficulty would be making a choice at all. We decided that we would be thrilled with any of the four and after losing Timber Creek, we didn't expect to get our first choice. Still, we had to start with one of them. So, which one? We were a little afraid to wait. Houses were flying off the market like hotcakes, but it was a big decision. We would all sleep on it and reconvene in the morning.

Morning came, and with it a discovery. Paula had been going through the listings with a fine-tooth comb and discovered that while all four had three bathrooms, Choice A had two full baths and one half while the rest had three full baths. It wasn't a deal breaker, but along with the general size of the place that moved it to the bottom of our list.

When you're choosing a place, you will be going through scads of listings. They're going to start blurring together. You're going to miss things. There were five of us scouring the listings, which was helpful, but it would have been even more helpful to show them to fresh eyes. When you narrow down the search you should show the listing to as many friends as possible. You'll make the final decision, it's your place after all, but their feedback will be invaluable.

How then to choose where to start? Maybe ask the one person with whom we could talk who'd seen the inside of these houses... Adam, realtor extraordinaire.

"House B," he said. "No, question." They were all nice, but in person, you could tell that C and D had been used a lot. Nothing terrible, just more wear and tear. B was pristine. We had to start somewhere and we might as well trust Adam. He represented all the houses and B wasn't the most expensive so it didn't seem like he was steering us there for a larger commission.

"Okay, let's do it," Francisco said to Adam. "What should we offer?"

"It's a very hot market and I'm showing it to another family today. I'd offer the asking price," Adam responded.

"Why don't you offer $10,000 below asking and see what they say," Francisco said.

My heart leapt to the back of my throat and then plunged to my bowels. This is why he was making the call. Both Anemone and I are much more likely to ask how much and then either pay that or walk away. Francisco would get us a better deal.

With the offer in, I boarded the bus back home. This time, I wouldn't get carried away. We'd put in an offer on one of the little yellow fairy houses, one of the houses I'd seen and remembered from years ago, one of the little yellow houses that had charmed Paula, Xanthus, and me so. Would this be our house?

It didn't hit me until I was lying in bed later that night. We were buying a house. I know it's a pretty common occurrence. People buy houses all the time. I'd been researching, saving, and planning for several years, but I don't think I thought it would be a reality. It felt like my blood was carbonated. I could barely lay still. I would have thought that once the offer had been made terror would descend on me like a raptor, but that didn't happen. There were so many things I didn't know, but I was prepared. I'd put in the work. It's a beautiful feeling to realize you have confidence in your ability to do something new.

The fluttery feeling subsided enough to let me fall asleep, only to reemerge the next morning. I was afraid we were going to lose the place right off the bat, but that's why I wasn't doing the negotiating. Besides, there were three other options if this fell through, and honestly, while I trusted Adam, Choice B wasn't my favorite.

Now we just had to wait.

We didn't have to wait long. Adam called back that afternoon. The owners had accepted our offer.

6

What's Inside

The negotiations had been blissfully easy. There was some thought and discussion that if the owners took our offer without countering, our offer must have been too high and we should have offered less. That might be true, but I was relieved. We didn't have a lot of money to work with. We were only putting 10 percent down and the houses were going quickly— many of them for cash offers. I was overjoyed we'd gotten a price we could afford. The only thing left to settle: which of the furnishings would the owners be taking with them? One of the reasons we'd been so taken with the Timber Creek property was that the listing said it came completely furnished.

If you're going to offer a short-term rental, it's going to have to be furnished. And not just furnished, you're going to want to offer abundance. So many short-term rentals give you two towels, one pot, limited cooking utensils, and a few other necessities. You don't want to be that host. Part of what differentiates short-term rentals from hotels is the way they're equipped. You want the guest to not only find anything they might need during their stay, you want them to feel like the house is packed with options and opportunities.

I had expected to buy an empty house, so I'd done extensive research and built up a spreadsheet with necessities and prices for each room. I'd wracked my brain, gone through my own rooms, and made lists— beds, linens, couch, table, kitchen essentials, etc., etc., etc. I'd come up with a total of about $15,000 to get a three-bedroom furnished with the basics. That was ridiculously low.

I do think we could have outfitted a house with the bare essentials for that. A lot of hosts do just that. It feels like that too— the bare minimum, a place to crash. That's okay I suppose, but you don't want that. You want to offer an experience. At least that's what we wanted.

Here we stumbled upon another stroke of luck. The houses in the little developments that lined the road leading to Mount Snow were vacation homes. Very few were permanent residences. People who own vacation homes don't want to sell their house and then have all of the furnishings moved somewhere and stored. So, most vacation homes come furnished. It wasn't just the Timber Creek property that came furnished. That was just the only one that had it in the listing. They all came furnished. Adam was getting a list of exceptions but we were getting a fully furnished house. I couldn't believe it. Even at the time, I was thinking it would save us $15,000. I would learn later that it would have probably cost us three times that to get the house to where we wanted. This should be a major consideration when you're selecting an area. A place full of vacation homes is likely to have some natural draw, but also, the houses are likely to come furnished. However much you think it will take to furnish a place, it will be more. Much more.

We pulled up the pictures and started ogling and listing our newfound treasures. The beds in the bedrooms looked fine. We would see about the mattresses. Each bedroom had an appropriate number of dressers and drawers, all tasteful, classic wood. The game room contained an enormous L-shaped couch that looked great, and a foosball table! It also had a large coffee table and a game cabinet. Atop the game cabinet a large flat-screen TV. The dining room had a classic country dining set seating six, and two bar stools for the counter. A stuffed moose head looked down over the three-sided fireplace into the den with two ugly plaid couches, a hideous red chair and ottoman, and that TV in the end of the counter. The master bedroom contained a mounted flat screen too, but surely, they would take the TVs with them. A grill sat on the deck along with a set of nice deck furniture. I wondered about the grill. They would probably take that. One thing I hadn't budgeted much for– decorations. The house was resplendent with paintings and wooden signs and various ski decorations. A lot of them seemed kind of tacky, but if they left them at least we'd have someplace to start and wouldn't have a house full of bare walls.

Another thing I'd forgotten in my spreadsheet— window dressing. Curtains and valances adorned all the windows, even a repugnant curtain to cover the sliding glass door that led to the deck. Again, I'd want to replace those soon, but it looked like we were in good shape to start.

When the list of exceptions arrived a few days later I expected it to be plump with furnishings that would not be ours. I joked with the family that I was fine with them taking anything else but if they took that moose head the deal was off! When we received the list, we found that they were taking two pictures that were drawn by the family and that silly stuffed moose.

7

The Window Is Closing

At the time, I'd never bought a house and I didn't quite know what to expect. Anemone and Francisco bought their first home a couple of years earlier. Not only that, they were both bankers. They would handle the mortgage and closing. We ended up going with one of the large banks they worked for. I do wish we'd gone with a local credit union, or at least a local bank. Turns out that would have saved us a little headache, not to mention, I love supporting local businesses, but we got an amazing rate from the big bank.

We should have started an LLC (limited liability company) and had the LLC buy the place with a DSCR loan. You can get a debt service cost ratio loan as long as your potential rental income exceeds your monthly expenses (i.e. mortgage, insurance, taxes, etc.), and if you put at least 20 percent down. This is a great way to buy a property that is going to be a business. It is better to have your property owned by an LLC for liability and tax reasons, but also because then each mortgage payment will increase the value of the business— value that you can borrow against for, say, another property. A DSCR loan is also great for a business because, with these loans, the lender doesn't even look at income or residency or any of the other things that can cause a hiccup when trying to buy an investment property with a traditional loan. However, we didn't know about these loans at the time. We didn't even have a registered LLC yet. The only way to buy a house, as far as we knew, was a personal mortgage. Not only were Anemone and Francisco the only ones with high-paying jobs, but at this point, they were the only ones with jobs period. The mortgage would have to be in their name. That's what they would put up for their equity in the business. Paula would put up Poppy and access to a twelve-month, 0 percent interest credit card. I would put up the lion's share of the money and a cash loan to the business, and Xanthus would put up a little cash and sweat equity.

The mortgage rates were historically low and we were able to get an unbelievably low interest rate even with only putting 10 percent down. Still, closing on a house takes time. The weeks dragged on. I was chomping at the bit to get started. It was exhilarating. It was terrifying. I felt the unseen weight of all that would need to be done.

Like most things in life, that weight loomed larger because it was unknown. I didn't even know, beyond the listing photos, what our new house would contain. With little I could do, I dove into data. I would learn as much as possible about the vacation rental market in our area. There are companies that will analyze the market for you and give you average prices and occupancy levels. We'd paid for a month of AirDNA, one of these companies, and I poured through it before making our offer on the house. That gave us a snapshot of the market, but I didn't think a snapshot was enough. Every day I would go onto Airbnb and pick through the listings in our little mountain village. I made note of how many three bedrooms were available on different dates. I made charts of their nightly rates and looked at availability on their calendars to try to get an idea of their occupancy levels. I scoured the listings, looked through hundreds of pictures, and made lists of what I liked and what I didn't. I jotted down any ideas that sprang to mind— decorating, amenities, and what made my eyes linger on a listing— anything that I thought might be helpful to us once we had possession of our house.

There are a lot of things you can't know just by looking at listings. Are the blocked-off dates booked nights? Or are they blocked off for the owners? You can see how much someone is asking for their place, but once it's blocked off on their calendar, you won't know how much the guests ended up paying for that stay. The more often you look, the more detail you're going to see. You will see when prices change. You'll see when properties are booked. I looked every day. I gathered data like a squirrel gathers nuts, manically and indiscriminately. More data points mean more accuracy and more accuracy means better predictability. Something else was happening. I was becoming an expert in the short-term rental market, at least in our region.

This is so important. It's easy to get wrapped up in your own place, but your place doesn't exist in a vacuum. You're competing with all the other properties available. You need to figure out what you can do better. What differentiates your property? You need to make your place stand out. Ironically, one of the best ways to do this is to look at as many listings as possible, and steal. Someone is going to come up with a great idea; something that you'd never think of– steal it. You'll make that idea your own. You'll make it unique to your place.

This is what I was doing while Anemone and Francisco battled mortgage brokers and bankers.

At some point along the line, Anemone called, "We have a closing date," she said.

November 6th. Money had to be moved around. Papers had to be signed. After weeks of waiting our lives exploded into a whirlwind of things that had to be done and done now! Anemone and Francisco steered us through these treacherous waters and it looked like smooth sailing. Then we hit a snag.

One last detail remained. The house had to be appraised for the bank to sign off on our mortgage. The real estate market had been on a steady rise for a while, but it exploded after our offer was accepted. Houses were selling like hotcakes and there weren't enough appraisers to go around, especially in southern Vermont. The earliest our appraiser could make it to our house, November 15th— a full week and a half after our closing date.

Not a big problem, right? We'd just have to wait a little bit longer to take possession.

Wrong. Houses were selling for 10, 15 percent more than just a couple of months ago. We had stumbled into making an offer at the perfect time. If we weren't ready to close on our closing date the sellers could void the deal. We'd lose good faith money, no paltry amount for us. But even worse we likely could no longer afford a house in the area. And why wouldn't the sellers back out? Houses were selling the same day they were listed. The sellers could get maybe $30,000–$40,000 more for their place.

We had to close on time.

Francisco hopped on the phone, calling all over trying to find an appraiser, but an available appraiser proved to be as elusive as Bigfoot. So how to have the house appraised in time? There seemed only one option: the age-old process of greasing the wheels of business with a little monetary lubricant. The appraisers in southern Vermont worked for themselves. It would only take a couple of hours to do the appraisal. No matter how busy they might be, surely one could find a few hours given the proper cash incentive.

We had maxed out our budget. We'd maxed out our budget and then some. I'd been socking money away for over a decade. It wasn't a lot though and not only was it my escape money, it was also my safety money.

The government had thrown me, along with more than 33 million other Americans, a lifeline in the form of enhanced unemployment insurance. I had a weekly unemployment payment along with the enhanced benefits. This money was keeping me, and countless Americans, from going under financially. It was keeping me above water. It wasn't enough to be funding a startup, and more importantly, it wasn't going to last forever.

Even more worrisome, I was a performer by trade and not just a performer, a live theater performer. When would people be able to gather in theaters again? What theaters would be left on the other side of the pandemic? Would my Met job survive the plague? Would any theater survive the plague? I pushed these thoughts to the back of my brain to add to the constant nagging ache of uncertainty.

There was another provision of the pandemic relief bill—if you had been furloughed you could withdraw money from your retirement savings without a tax penalty. That's what I did. Writing this now I don't know if it was courage, stupidity, or confidence. It was probably a healthy mix of all three, but we had some more capital and we could slip an appraiser some extra money to get a rush job –right?

Wrong.

We weren't hiring the appraiser. Our bank was hiring the appraiser. The whole point of the appraiser was to protect the bank, to make sure that the mortgage was congruent with the value of the house. It was illegal for us to offer extra money to the appraiser. It would look like a bribe to inflate the value of the house.

It was worse than just that, though. We weren't even allowed to contact the appraiser. How could it be so hard to bribe someone? We didn't want the appraiser to give an artificial or inflated evaluation. We just wanted them to come and give an honest report before our closing date. All kidding aside we were thinking of it as an extra inconvenience fee, like if you have to call a plumber on Christmas Eve. You better believe that plumber is going to be more expensive. Our thinking was that even if the appraiser's schedule was booked full, for enough money he would work late. If only we could figure out a way to contact him. Francisco started calling around. I made a mental note to look into how one gets an appraiser's license. It seemed like an in-demand career. I'm not sure how Francisco did it, but he got us an appraisal date. A regular appraisal in that area runs about $500. We would pay $2,500. Does that sound like a lot? Just between you and me at that point, I would have paid double just to close on the house.

Back on the phone with Adam, Francisco explained that we indeed would have an appraisal– on the day of closing.

"Yes," he said. "That would probably work."

And just like that, it was ours. Our family-owned a house in southern Vermont.

8

Funding

We'd gotten our place with 10percent down. Even so, it had taken all the money we could scrape together. I loaned the business an extra $15,000 to get us through closing and then another $8,000 for incidentals. Our closing costs covered all of our expenses through December 31st, 2020.

I was tapped out. I'd put in more than twice what I had expected. Xanthus had put in all the money he had. We all had good credit. That was invaluable in many ways. Anemone and Francisco's credit snagged us a mortgage rate of 2.75 percent. Even with the mortgage insurance, we would have to pay for only putting 10 percent down, that low rate made our monthly payments manageable– at least according to my improvised business plan.

Paula's good credit equaled a new credit card for the business with twelve months of 0 percent interest on purchases.

That credit card provided us with a little cushion. I wouldn't necessarily recommend credit cards as a funding option. A lot of startups do it, still, it's risky business. After those twelve months, the card would start to hammer us with 20+ percent interest. I think we could have done it without the credit card. Maybe. The house came furnished and we probably could have made do with what was on hand.

Life has taught me these two lessons over and over— there is a limit to how many corners you can cut and still do something right. If you don't do it right, you are not going to succeed.

Money had always been tight. So many projects I'd attempted during my life failed for lack of commitment– mostly a lack of financial commitment. I'd tried doing things on the cheap, or cutting corners, or just hedging. I wasn't going to do that this time. I was going to do what was necessary to give us the best chance of success.

We closed on November 6th, 2020.

On January 1st, 2021, our first mortgage payment would be due. Three months of HOA fees, no small amount, would be due. Propane to heat a large house in Vermont in the winter, electricity, and credit card minimum payments would all be due.

We had nothing in the bank. We had a house in Vermont. We had a tiger by the tail.

9

Numbers

When I first started looking at houses, I instantly rejected any properties with HOA (home owners association) fees. It just seemed wasteful. It seemed like a huge unnecessary monthly expense. Holy bejeezus was I mistaken. When our realtor told us we really needed to be on the Mount Snow road if we wanted to rent our place the chance of no HOA disappeared. All of the properties along that road were communities and they all had HOA fees; some more than others.

The Kingswood HOA— a whopping $750 a month. I balked pretty hard at that. Surely, we could take care of the place ourselves for much cheaper. It was a moot point though; I loved the house and there was no option. That HOA proved to be worth every cent.

First off, there's a sports center, complete with an Olympic-size pool and exercise room (and staff). That's practically worth it right there. A beautiful indoor pool that you don't have to clean, maintain, or take care of in any way? Yes, please. Then there's that magical landscape I was telling you about. As magical as it looks, it doesn't just happen magically. It does for us, though, with the HOA that is. Free, fresh wood that just appears stacked nice and neat next to our front door. That's courtesy of the HOA. And the snow, oh lordie, lordie, the snow. The roads and walkways are always freshly plowed the morning after a snowstorm.

That $750 a month may be the best bargain I've ever found. HOAs aren't always going to be a possibility and they certainly aren't all good, but if you're looking for a short-term rental property, they are something you should consider, especially if you are going to be a distance owner. There will be plenty else for you to do.

While we're talking funding, let's talk numbers a little bit. I'm always surprised how many businesses fail because their owners jump in armed only with some sort of vague hope. The beautiful thing about numbers is that they are, by definition, quantifiable. There are so many unknowns when starting a new business. It always seems weird that someone wouldn't want as many solid facts on which to base their decisions as possible.

To start, you want two numbers: a yearly operating budget and a startup budget. You need to do that before you buy a property. It's not like buying a home. It's not just a matter of what you can afford based on a down payment; you need to have an idea of your rental potential. You're going to be preapproved for either a mortgage or a business loan (unless you're lucky enough to do a cash deal). So how do you figure these two potentially ephemeral numbers?

You know how many days there are in a year. You know how many weekends. You can get an idea of how much other properties in the area are charging per night, weekends, high season, low season, etc. and you can get an idea of their occupancy levels. The more listings you watch and the longer you watch them the more accurate your numbers will be.

Figure out the average nightly rates, both weekday and weekend, for properties similar to the ones you're looking to buy. Once you have the average rate for the different times of year for properties like yours, add it all up. Is this the maximum you could expect to earn if you run the property perfectly?

No, not yet. You're going to have to do turnovers in between unless you think you can do a same-day turn. More on that later. A better way is to use the average occupancy rate. There are companies that will give you the occupancy rate for your area, for a fee. The average occupancy rate for Airbnb worldwide is 18 percent. Don't panic. That doesn't take into account the fact that most short-term rentals aren't available 365 days a year. People rent out their place when they aren't using the places themselves or when they're away on vacation or business travel or a myriad of other reasons.

The average rate for properties that are full-time short-term rentals is 47 percent That's still not great, right? First, you can make even that profitable. Second, you're not going to be average, are you? We're going to help you increase that rate. But don't assume that you're going to be a rock star right out of the gate. Personally, I wouldn't even assume that you're going to hit average when figuring your budget. I used 40 percent.

So, add the average rates for comparable properties in the area, then multiply those times 0.4. If you think you'll hit 40 percent occupancy, that should be your ceiling for the yearly operating budget.

What's included in your operating budget? The big one is probably going to be your mortgage, but we're going to reverse-engineer what you can afford to spend on that.

Start with utilities— your electricity, heat, internet, cable, water. Add those up and multiply by twelve for your yearly utilities. Some of these will vary depending on the number of guests, but you can get a general idea. What about outside maintenance? Lawn care, gardening, trash pickup, snow shoveling. Our HOA took care of the outside maintenance, maybe yours will too. Add all of these up.

That number plus your mortgage is your fixed cost– the amount that it costs just to have your place whether someone is renting or not.

Now you need your variable costs. Cleaning– will you do that yourself? We did, at least to start. You can save a lot that way. Amenities— we'll talk about that in a later chapter, but once you know what amenities you're going to offer and how much they cost, you'll want a per-booking amenity cost. Multiply that by the number of guests you expect per year based on that 40 percent occupancy. "What if we have more guests?" you may ask. Any additional guests will bring in additional revenue, so if your expense model is sound, they will take care of themselves.

There will be more operating costs as you grow, but right now you're just trying to figure out your base levels, so you only need two more numbers: your mortgage and a figure for unexpected expenses. For unexpected expenses, I use 2 percent of the Yearly Operating Budget number. Take the YOB x .02 = Unexpected Expenses. Now add Fixed Costs+Per Booking Costs+Unexpected Expenses. Take that number and subtract it from your YOB, divide that number by twelve, and that's what you can afford to spend on your mortgage.

Sure, maybe you can do better, but you'll be a lot happier and certainly less stressed if you can make your expenses every month without worry.

I had run all of these numbers and tracked the Airbnb trends for months, nay, years. Our mortgage fit in the formula. Our start-up costs had been higher than expected, but still, we should be okay. I'd figured out our budget on the conservative side. We should be fine. It's all fine and good figuring it all out on paper,

ZEPHYRUS WHITE

but when it's the first time, the fact that this was all theoretical weighed on my shoulders like the weight of the house itself.

10

What's in a Name?

If you choose to enter the STR market, you will be running a business. Make no mistake on that point. You are in the hospitality business. A lot of people are going to think they're just renting out a house. No, you're renting out an experience. The good news? There is a lot of information about business and marketing out there. The bad news? It can feel like a Sisyphean task sifting through all of the bad info just to find the gems. So how do you decide what information is viable? Where do you look to learn?

The internet is your friend. Not your calm, reasonable, well-thought-out friend, though. The internet is more like your ADD-addled, genius friend who's always bouncing from one hair-brained idea to another. There's some great info out there but you're going to have to do a lot of sifting. The first thing to look for? Does the information sound simple? Is the purveyor boasting amazing results? Run. Those aren't for you. Most things worthwhile aren't simple, they're not easy. And they don't pay huge dividends for little work. There are scads of gurus out there telling you about all the passive income you can make in the short-term rental market. It may become passive at some point, but for a while, it's going to be anything but.

Do you know what you don't know? That's the biggest challenge I've found. If there's something specific you need to learn, that's not so hard these days. But how do you know what you need to know? This is where the pandemic gave me a bit of a gift. I had no real business background. I'd been an artist all my life. I did run my career like a business. I credit a lot of my success in theater to just that.

Well, it's not exactly true that I had *no* business experience. My family has always had a strong entrepreneurial bent. Always enthusiastic. Rarely successful. My parents had been doing side hustles before side hustles were even a thing, and as a kid, I'd started a rash of little businesses myself.

At age five, I'd taken a tin of peppermint sticks that my mom received as a gift and started selling them door to door. She'd said she didn't like them so I figured best make use of the candy. I still can't believe I did that. I was terribly shy, but I must have needed money for something.

At age nine, I opened a pet store stocked solely with turtles and snakes that I caught in fields and ponds. I might have made a go of it too, if my stand hadn't been on a country road with only a couple of cattle trucks coming by each day.

I'd had a bunch of little enterprises like that, but all of my business knowledge was cobbled together from common sense and what I'd gleaned throughout the years. I didn't have a framework. So now that it was time to learn about business, where to look? Do you know who can teach you about business? Harvard Business School. Do you know who went entirely online during the pandemic? Harvard Business School.

Let me share with you a story about an almost-forgotten dream coming true. I suppose I should start by acknowledging that I've been pretty lucky in the dreams-come-true department. If you traveled back in time to Kansas, and found little eleven-year-old Zephyrus, probably sitting in a tree daydreaming, and told him that someday he'd travel the world, live in New York City, make his living in the theater, not only love but be loved by some truly incredible women, jump out of planes, fly a helicopter, climb mountains, ride motorcycles, swim with sea turtles... well, that little eleven-year-old would probably fall right out of that tree. Maybe not, I was a hopeful little cuss.

But those aren't the dreams I want to tell you about today. Back when I was a wee lad I was obsessed with Einstein. Loved him. He made sense of the world and that was something I was in desperate need of. I used to go to our little library and read all about him. Now, Einstein won the Nobel Prize. Back then I was really into validation and the Nobel Prize seemed like the ultimate validation. (Spoiler alert: This little story does *not* end with me winning the Nobel Prize.)

I used to pour over those encyclopedias and read about Nobel Prize winners and statistics. You know what kept popping up? Harvard University. A disproportionate number of the winners went to Harvard. For some reason that clicked. Harvard was the place for me. I know what you're thinking, Einstein's a Princeton man, so why didn't you want to go to Princeton? Who can know how the mind of an eleven-year-old boy works?

Now, there was no way a poor kid from the Midwest was going to Harvard. I knew that, but the thought lodged in the back of my mind. I always thought of Harvard as, I don't know, perhaps the road not taken; the maybe in another life, dream.

Now I needed to learn about business. I started looking at Coursera and other online offerings. Arden (you'll meet her later) said, "Why don't you just apply to Harvard Business School? They're offering certificate programs online."

At the time the world was upside down. Why wouldn't I apply? It only cost me some time for the application and a paltry $25 application fee. Besides, then I could say I applied to Harvard University. That would be cool. I wrote the essay, filled out the forms, submitted them, and promptly forgot about the whole thing. A few weeks later, an official-looking letter came in the mail. It was an acceptance letter to a program for entrepreneurs and small business owners offered by Harvard Business School.

It was a certificate program. I wouldn't be getting an MBA from Harvard and it's a distance learning course, so I wouldn't be wandering around Harvard Yard, but I ended up with HBS credits on my transcript, a Harvard ID in my wallet, and some Harvard knowledge in my head. Even now, the thought of that makes the eleven-year-old boy in me giddy.

So now I had a little business knowledge, and some of that included the basics of marketing. I knew I'd need to learn more on that front, but I had a foundation, and that's where we'd start.

If you're going to promote your property, you're going to need a brand. Not only for promotional purposes, but if you're building a consistent brand, that will inform much of what you do: the kind of decorations you use, the way you write your descriptions, and even your interactions with your guests. We didn't know the intricacies of building a brand at that time. We did know our little yellow house needed a name.

If you look on Airbnb or Vrbo, most of the houses you will see won't have names. How do you remember them? How do you tell your friends about them? Sure, you can say, "You know the one with the cool bathroom," or "The one with the blue door," or whatever. Any description is going to be subjective. Do you know what's not subjective? A name. If your house has a name, it's on the way to having a personality. Personalities are enticing, they're evocative, they are memorable. Our house needed a name.

We sat around the dining room table at my sister's place and brainstormed. The house was whimsical. The house was unique. The house was yellow. We all tossed out ideas, but Anemone hit the jackpot.

"What about the Lemondrop Lodge?"

That was it. There wasn't any discussion. The name was perfect. You know those kid's toys with differently shaped blocks and matching holes? When you pick up the star block and slide it into the star hole– it's just right. That's how the name felt. What did it mean? I don't know. The house was yellow, and lemons are yellow. "Lemondrop" sounded kind of like something from fairyland, which is what the Kingswood community felt like to me. Lemondrop the drink brings to mind a kind of elevated experience. "Lodge" felt right for a ski town, plus who doesn't love alliteration?

Our house had a name. We were the proud owners of the Lemondrop Lodge.

11

There's No Escape. Or Is There?

The anticipation felt like a balloon filling slowly with the air of time. I was about to burst. It wasn't just the two months of waiting to close. I'd been thinking about this for upward of five years. Now it was November. All the papers were signed. All the money was transferred. The t's crossed the i's dotted. Wednesday morning, I made the journey from my apartment in New York City to my family out in New Jersey. I donned gloves and masks on the bus then stripped down and changed in their backyard, goosebumps from the cold blooming alongside the goosebumps of excitement.

We had no firm plan, and we'd done all that we could before actually seeing our house, but I didn't want to be alone. I wanted to be with the family and share the moments.

Today was Wednesday. The keys would be ours on Friday. Nothing left to do for the next two days but dream– dream and maybe some yard work in New Jersey on the crisp fall morning.

Everything was still pretty much shut down, with the exception of essential businesses such as grocery stores, hospitals, police, and banks. Anemone and Francisco never stopped working. Francisco's work shifted to mostly remote, but Anemone went into her bank every day. She was meticulous. Every time she came home, she would change into a robe in the vestibule, put her work clothes in a plastic bag, and then go immediately upstairs and shower before talking to anyone. It may seem like a bit of overkill now. Back then it seemed only reasonable. She was forward-facing at work with a flood of people to deal with every day. One thing we would learn during the pandemic, the virus comes for us all eventually. It came for her that Wednesday.

Paula, Xanthus, and I passed the morning in the backyard talking, dreaming, and raking leaves. About midafternoon Anemone's car pulled into the driveway. I started forward to talk about the new house. She waved me off before I got to their little white picket fence.

"I'm not feeling well," she said over the fence from a safe distance. "I don't think it's Covid, but better not come closer. I'm going to go upstairs and rest."

A few hours later and Francisco wasn't feeling well either. This was way before there were home tests available to the general public, so they headed to the medical clinic to try and to a Covid test.

Just between you and me, I wasn't all that scared of getting Covid myself. I've always been pretty healthy; I didn't have any risk factors and illnesses never hit me particularly hard– same thing for Xanthus. I was worried about Paula though. She is also very healthy and didn't have any risk factors, but she was in her seventies. Throughout the whole pandemic, my biggest health fear was that I would get Covid and pass it to someone who would get very sick or even die from my infection. This was still during the time when no one was allowed in a hospital except the patient– the patient if they were lucky. People were going into the hospitals feeling just a little ill and then going on ventilators and never seeing their family or loved ones again. I was afraid of that for my mother.

So, what to do? Anemone and Francisco could stay on the second floor. Their two kids, four and five? Paula could take care of them, but what if the kids were already infected? They had definitely been exposed to their parents and were likely carrying the virus. Should Paula be taking care of them? That Wednesday night I went back to New York. Paula quarantined down to the basement, Xanthus stayed on the main floor, and Francisco, Anemone, and the two kids went upstairs. This wasn't a viable solution. Something would have to be done.

Xanthus and Paula spent a significant portion of the next day standing in line to get tested. Negative for both of them. Two positive cases, two negative cases, and two kids. What to do....

No small part of our strength as a business lies in our diversity. I think that is also part of what makes our story so relatable. No matter who you are, there is probably one of us with whom you can identify. So, to that end, I'm going to let Paula tell the next part of the story in her own words.

12

Paula's Story

Fall of 2020, the pandemic was at its height. The kid's preschool was closed, and they didn't get out much at all. Even our park was closed. I was creative keeping them active, involved, and experiencing life. Everyone was concerned about me catching Covid, being the over seventy-year-old of the bunch, even though I had no compromising conditions.

The stories had put a fear in us— going to the hospital and never seeing loved ones again. Then the inevitable happened just after Halloween. Both Francisco and Anemone got sick – Yup, it was Covid. The family worried about me because there was no real way to quarantine inside our home. Xanthus and I went the next morning to be tested. After waiting in line for a couple hours we both tested negative. We would have to leave the house. Where could we go? A hotel? That seemed expensive and far from ideal. Then eureka! It was Thursday. On Friday, we would take possession of the Lemondrop Lodge, although we had not yet arranged how we would get the keys. We could go there!

We only had to stay in the basement for the rest of the day and another night. Then we could leave. A call to Adam told us that the keys would be under the bear paw metal piece on the front step. We, of course, had not seen the house at all except for pictures. We had no idea what would be there, except for the furniture we saw in the listing pictures. I spent Thursday afternoon gathering cleaning supplies, packing books and projects to work on, and every essential thing I thought we might need in our retreat to Vermont. Xanthus gathered food to cook.

We were not supposed to go to Vermont. We certainly weren't supposed to go to stores or restaurants. Anemone put in an order to Whole Foods to be delivered to the porch early on Friday morning for us to take. We were unsure just how long we'd be gone. It was sort of ominous, and yet I was filled with an excitement I hadn't felt in a long time. It would be an adventure. Zephyrus would be left behind in his Manhattan apartment but would be close enough to come to the aid of the Covid stricken and the kids if need be. It was difficult to leave them knowing not only the difficulty of being sick, but also having to care for a five-year-old and four-year-old. Plus, Xanthus and I both felt a little awkward to be the first to see the Lemondrop Lodge. We had hoped we could all go together. In retrospect, it was a gift to have that time for me and Xanthus to sort through, clean, and ready the Lemondrop Lodge.

We drove out of the driveway, car full, once again in faithful Poppy, our New Jersey plates evident. Would anyone question why we were there in Vermont? Many thoughts filled our minds, from those we left behind to what awaited us in Vermont. We were full of excitement as well as concern. Would the Lemondrop Lodge meet our expectations? Would we be allowed into the state? There were no checkpoints as we crossed the New York-Vermont border. We just noticed the smooth road and the incredible scenery. Fall colors had come and gone, but there was a calming beauty to behold. Three and a half hours after we pulled out of our New Jersey driveway and, as we turned into the Kingswood community, we experienced such a high of emotions. One of these yellow houses in this magical village was now ours. Would we be happy with it when we saw it for real? Was that a bit of fear lurking behind the highs? Would we be able to convey to the others how it looked? Could we enjoy the excitement knowing two of our family were sick with the dreaded Covid and one was glued to his computer studying Airbnb listings and short-term rentals while we were first through the door?

We slowly pulled into the driveway the reality right in front of us. There it was. We had seen it from the outside on that quick trip up. What if the keys weren't there? We had never met the realtor. We didn't even know where his office was and couldn't go there if we did.

The day was sunny. The air was fresh and crisp. The whimsical house beckoned us toward the door. I turned on my camera and started to film as we approached our door. There it was just as it was supposed to be: the bear paw. Xanthus lifted the paw and there they were: our keys, signifying ownership of, and permission to finally enter, the Lemondrop Lodge.

Opening that white door with the French windows was the actual beginning of an incredible adventure our family had only dreamed about. We had poured over the pictures of the place, but that couldn't compare to actually walking in and seeing it in person. Here it was.

Looking down over the ledge to the living room was a total high. That glimpse reminded me of looking over the balcony railing to the living room when I was a child. My childhood home, which was built and designed by my parents, was a bit ahead of its time in the open concept. We walked through the three levels and looked in every room and behind every door; it was just amazing. We knew we were buying a furnished home, but we had no idea just what all the hidden furnishings would be. The closets and drawers were filled with treasurers. As we walked through, we would both squeal, from different rooms, our delight in the findings. There was a foosball table. There was not just one, but two vacuums— we could clean. They left all three TVs. They left dishes, pots and pans, lots of cleaning supplies, and on and on.

We had to figure out the light switches and dimmers. Was the heat on? There were two thermostats. We looked in the utility room and made a mental note to check all those devices. More extras there— light bulbs, tools, a bucket, and an umbrella for the deck table. We plugged in the refrigerator. Yes, it worked. Great, we needed to get all our food supplies in the fridge.

Then out the patio door to check the deck and our backyard. To our surprise, we found the owners had left the grill, and it was in good shape.

We had to make ourselves stop the discovery phase and place a call to those left behind to announce we not only made it and got inside but we were in love with the Lemondrop Lodge. It topped our expectations. We reported that it was clean and filled with things we needed.

We were coming down from the high a bit and found we were hungry and needed to eat. We had driven through the main street as we came in. But we knew we couldn't go to any of the restaurants even if they were open. We noted a 7-Eleven where we could go for gas. Though I am the mama, as my kids became adults, they became the cooks of the family. My focus would be to clean, sort, and make lists. Xanthus would keep us fed as well as look to techno questions and do the heavy lifting and cleaning.

We beamed at each other with wide smiles, reveling in this incredible home that was now ours, and ate our sandwiches, mostly quiet, taking in the magic of the moment. We had just acquired a condo in the mountains of Vermont and were entering the short-term rental business. Fortified by food, we unpacked the rest of the car, letting our possessions further claim this fairy house as ours.

Prior to moving to New Jersey to be with my family, I managed a charity thrift shop for thirteen years. Those years at the thrift shop had given me a lot of skills— among them the ability to quickly sort through accumulations of all kinds of items, determining worth and value, what could be cleaned and repurposed, and what wouldn't make muster. I am a list maker. So out came my always present legal pads, color coordinated: one for measurements and other info to send back to those at home, one for what-do-we-need, another for the tasks at hand that needed to be done as we discovered them. We loosely set up sorting stations to begin our triage of the contents of the Lemondrop Lodge.

One of our first orders of business was to find out the size of our mattresses. Of course, I had brought measuring tapes, and the internet supplied the measurements of different size mattresses. We called this info back home. Even though Anemone was sick with Covid, she had started designing the bedrooms; color, linens, and all the accessories we would need to set up the bedrooms.

I already knew of and admired Anemone's creative, crafty skills, but I would soon learn that bedroom design was also one of her areas of expertise. She excelled at bringing life to her visions as well as the ability to find great bargains in the process.

I could only imagine the welcoming beauty the bedrooms would offer when she finished her preparations.

We figured we needed all new linens. Though there were a few mismatched sheets, pillows, spreads, and blankets, most of them we had to just trash. There were a lot of pillows in various states of quality— We sorted them, threw some, and put a few replacements and pillow protectors on our list, until we could buy all new. To get our listing up quickly, the bedrooms had to be ready.

After eating and unpacking, Xanthus and I began a slower, go-through, of the house. This time, we went through with a more critical eye, looking a little deeper and with more care. We found that though the first impression was awesome, we realized that this condo had been a vacation home and not been used often; we began to see the accumulation of dust, grime, some neglect, and the need for a real deep cleaning everywhere.

If you looked at Xanthus's or my living quarters, you might not have chosen us to render the Lemondrop shipshape. We are not obsessive in cleaning our places— but this was different. We were going to not only invite guests into the Lemondrop Lodge, we were going to ask them to pay for the experience. That would require white-glove cleaning and care, and we were more than capable of that.

It became evident quickly that we were in the hospitality business. Xanthus who has worked in the high-end restaurant business in New York City for twenty years, was maybe the first to embrace that thought. Our guests were going to spend their hard-earned money to gain a memorable vacation and we wanted to give them just that. I found, as time went on, that Xanthus had a gift for ferreting out those places needing attention and getting them in shape.

We enjoyed the rest of that first day, going piecemeal through the house, and found we were exhausted. I had fallen in love with the white/winter room with its castle-round windows that let in sunlight, which I love, and claimed as my room for sleeping. Xanthus, who has almost always found couches preferable to beds, wanted to bunk on the large L-shaped couch in the den with the large TV.

Upon waking in the morning, we hesitantly checked in with each other. How did we feel? After all, we had been exposed, no matter how minimally, to the dread Covid. Each of those first mornings, that is how we began. After a few days, we began to feel secure that we had escaped the virus this time. We set about in earnest and with more of a plan. We would need to use the kitchen to fix our food, so it seemed sensible to start there. A cupboard at a time, we cleaned inside and out. Xanthus and I pondered over things like utensils, pots and pans, dishes, etc. What to keep, what would we still need, and what was obvious trash?

Searching for the dishwasher instruction book took me to the miscellaneous drawer. It was a goldmine. Thanks to the former owners. They had kept instruction manuals for almost everything in the house. When I needed a break from the up and down of cleaning, I would sit in what became my favorite chair and pour over all the instruction manuals for details.

It's funny now to think about the burgundy, semi-wing back chair in the living room. We, of course, saw it in the pictures. Most of us were kind of repulsed by it and said that would have to go right away. To me, it looked red; I do not like red. It looked velvety, and that seemed shabby. The first time I took a break from cleaning I gravitated to that chair, seeking the sun coming in the patio door for light. While sitting in the chair, the ottoman made a perfect little desk to hold the manuals and my legal pads for notes. By that first night's end, when some of those manual searches turned into longer rest periods, snuggling back into the chair, with my hurt knee, tired legs, and feet supported by the ottoman, I found I had fallen in love with it. I decided then and there, if everyone else still wanted to trash this chair, it was coming home with me. Next to the patio drapes, with their hint of burgundy and the burgundy stripe on the couch, the red had faded and paled to burgundy, which I'm quite fond of. When I shared that news with Zephyrus by phone, he was very skeptical, but once he made it to Lemondrop in person and sat in the chair it became a favorite of his too. The chair stayed in the Lemondrop. Pictures can be deceiving.

As the second evening approached our bodies were tired and achy, our minds were fried from excitement, and the list of to-dos we were making had grown longer. We found ourselves longing for some of Xanthus' soup and a good movie and popcorn. Xanthus's with his observant eye mused that he had seen a Redbox video rental at the 7-Eleven— outside. And it so happened our former owners left a DVD player.

I was game for a ride into town to at least look at the movie options. How could we get in trouble for standing outside choosing a movie? We would mask up. What a trip back in time to choose a movie, actually two, from a Redbox. We were in rural Vermont during the pandemic. This was an adventure, and we would utilize what was available like pioneers. Soon we were snuggled up on the large blue couch in the den eating popcorn and watching a movie in our newly purchased townhome, the Lemondrop Lodge. It was a perfect, relaxing evening that felt full of the promise of excitement and adventure.

Back home, as we were relaxing, Zephyrus was diligently navigating the Airbnb listing website and all of its maze-like qualities. He texted us detailed questions about the Lemondrop so he could fill in the boxes and options on the listing. It was now November 8th. Ski season was nearly upon us. It was crucial we get Lemondrop ready for guests and our listing live. He would share details he was learning as he worked relentlessly to get the listing ready. It became more apparent to me what a massive, detailed, intertwined, and potentially flummoxing mission he was on. I pondered this elder son of mine. His life had been filled with adventures and dreams of one kind or another, and he had so generously shared them with me over the years, the highs and the lows. How clear it was to me that each adventure or new path, success or not, had been preparing him in one way or another for this leap into home ownership and the STR business. I am so proud of Zephyrus and all he has overcome, worked through, and persevered through. I remembered a framed poem in my belongings:

> *"Come to the edge."* Life said.
> They said: *"We are afraid."*
> *"Come to the edge."* Life said.
> They came. It pushed them....
> and they Flew.

~ Guilliaume Apollinaire.

Zephyrus had come to the edge but Zephyrus was now flying and taking us all for a ride. It was exhilarating. I was ever so confident Zephyrus would get that listing ready that it would be and one of the best ever.

By day three, refreshed from movie night and a great night's sleep, we were ready to really make progress.

We would need a long dusting wand to reach the high ceiling fans. They were very dusty.

I took apart the two vacuums, learned their details, cleaned them well, and noted the numbers for ordering new filters. We checked and counted carbon monoxide detectors and smoke alarms to see if we had enough to adhere to the state requirements.

The stove was a glass top. I had never cooked on one or cleaned one or wished to have one before. But have one we did. So off to the instruction manual I went. I learned a lot. Amazing. I would have to use a razor blade to scrape off caked-on spills. It was important to know the authentic way to clean this stove. I found that we could get special sprays, wipes, brushes, and cream to use in different ways. On the shopping list, they went.

Yea! There was a garbage disposal and it worked. Ice and baking soda went in it to clean and deodorize.

We were still periodically running dishes through the dishwasher. I was glad to have the forethought to bring a bag of cleaner pods. We nestled our newly purchased IKEA set of dishes in the cabinet next to the old-fashioned red barn dishes— a set of twelve. They seemed a little odd but they have grown on us and some of our guests seem to prefer them. We had begun our big pile of discards. I looked up how to get to the Kingswood garbage dump and how to sort trash and recyclables. It was time for an excursion to the dump to rid the kitchen area of a carload of trash. It is important in these mountains of Vermont to not leave any garbage outside that would attract the black bears who live in these parts. The dumpsters were well within a nice walk if you only had a sack or two, but on this trip, we would be driving carloads. The dump was a large trash receptacle within a fenced surrounding. You could start the crusher. There was a separate trash receptacle for all things recyclable.

This had been the former owner's vacation home for many years, not a rental. Like most of us in a long-term home, we collect things that we probably should have thrown away. I suppose since they were selling it furnished, it didn't occur to them to put in a lot of effort to sort through it. And that mindset was a gift to us, as so much of what they left was useful. But we did need to sort and decide what we might be willing to live with, even if it was just until we could find or afford something better.

Now we were in the hospitality business and our concern had to be for our guests and what kind of kitchen or home we wanted to offer to them. What would we be proud to present? We became more selective going through the cupboards a second time. It was plain to see we had to invest in a set of cookware. We had already bought a set of dishes, flatware for twelve, glasses, and some stemware. We kept some of the interesting coffee cups and commemorative glasses. We decided that interesting coffee cups would be something we'd try to expand upon. To start we left our Kansas tornado cup. We took inventory and texted Zephyrus everything we could count.

We sorted things on the counter and made a list: a new toaster and coffee maker were a must.

Needing a break from the kitchen I headed to the bathrooms. We had three to clean. Xanthus decided it was time to vacuum and deep clean the big blue L-shaped couch in the den and check out its viability as a sleeper sofa. If we were going to list our place as sleeping eight it was a necessity to determine if the couch would be an adequate sleeping option for our guests. We decided in the end that it could be, but we may need to invest in a new mattress down the line.

Even though at first glance, the house certainly wasn't trashed or messy, it had been empty and not carefully cleaned for a long time. This was during the pandemic and searches online and the Airbnb site said cleanliness was the top concern of those searching for a place to stay. Airbnb also had a cleaning Covid protocol that you could promise to use and it would be noted on your listing. That sounded important to us. So that was a lot of reading, researching, and making notes in the burgundy chair for me. Lots of Lysol and attention to all places where fingers touched for Xanthus. But mostly it was cleaning that you would want to do anyway.

Bathrooms we decided were a place to gain the respect and appreciation of guests for the cleanliness of our Home. A little dust on the mantle was one thing but soap scum in the bathtub or dried urine on the toilet seat crevices, or a long hair in the tub, or smudges on the mirror was quite another. If the bathrooms shined, the guests would know we took cleaning seriously and more likely could overlook some minor issue elsewhere should it occur. Toilets are a particular concern of mine. They must be immaculate. I quickly found an old toothbrush in a drawer and used it to scrub. I needed to remove the toilet seat to clean the years of accumulated yuk. All the while cleaning we were thinking of what amenities we would offer– definitely not bar soap– too wasteful and leaves too much residue to clean. We wanted our guests to be able to find what they needed and maybe had forgotten. We wanted to pamper them. We asked ourselves - What did we want when we stayed overnight somewhere? What had we forgotten that made our experience a little less enjoyable?

I have been cleaning for over sixty-five years and I do have my favorite cleaning supplies and can tell if something works or not.

Even though it was November in Vermont, the days were sunny and fairly warm inviting me outside to enjoy the fresh, peaceful tranquil surroundings. It was calm— a calm still foreign to me after thirty-plus years in Kansas where a calm day is as rare as a white elephant. We had opened all the windows and turned on the ceiling fans to clear the stale air and fill the house with the freshness of the Vermont fall.

Sure, it would move the dust around, but vacuuming and dusting would come in the days to come. I decided the windows and screens needed washing. I took the screens outside with a bucket of sudsy water and scrub brush— yes, they were dirty. We only had a small five-foot ladder which helped on the lower windows but on the top floor, I just reached out as best I could. The screens were held in place by a little swivel screw jobby that I had never seen before. Most were there but we'd have to find some replacements. Two years later, we're still hunting for them.

Our work was kind of in layers after that. After that first impression, where everything looked pretty darn good, we continually found things to throw away. Some pillows had to go, as well as bathroom rugs. Some utensils and pots and pans in the kitchen just couldn't pass the test of what we wanted to provide for our guests. We were also continually amazed at the found treasures and practical things that were going to save us a lot of money. We had never even thought of finding a furnished place to buy. But now in the middle of the task of getting it ready, it seemed it would have been overwhelming to decide what kind of furniture, color scheme, and decor and reach a consensus between all five of us. Now we had a framework within which to work. Even though there were things that none of us would have chosen, they would suffice to get us listed and up and going.

It was the pandemic. People were leaving home and working remotely. The internet was crucial and we didn't have it. While television may not be important to everyone, we were sure that guests having skied all day would want some rest in front of the TV at night. Xanthus checked the internet, called around and finally found the answer in a satellite antenna. He got that arranged, and even got an appointment on the fourth day of our arrival.

We knew other condos had satellites on the roof, but after checking the HOA rules, we found they could not be installed on the roof. The workman found a place, and up it went. Again, we were grateful for the credit card.

Xanthus also worked on the grill and deck, taking stock and cleaning. He is the techno guy so he set about investigating the three TVs, all of which were rather dated. He decided on what we would need to get them fully operational.

After more of Xanthus's food, another movie and sleep with the fresh Vermont air to breathe, we were back at it again, early the next morning— another trip to the dump. It was within walking distance— a little jaunt but doable with one of two bags. We had the backend of Poppy, with seats folded down, filled. When I remember how tidy and uncluttered the townhome seemed when we first entered, it was hard to imagine now that we took four full loads to the trash area during that stay. It was all neatly packed away in drawers, closets, and cupboards, I guess.

Xanthus and I had gone to IKEA and bought a set of dishes, flatware, glasses, etc. We figured we would need them and we thought we could set up the table and take some pictures for the listing. It looked beautiful. Perhaps no one on a ski weekend would opt for a formal dinner, but the pictures showed that it was possible in our home and that we had everything needed.

I kept thinking that surely we would see some black bears. No, not even one. Though the thought of going for a walk after dark was hard to imagine. It was pitch black and how would you see a bear? The warnings were evident not to leave any garbage or especially food outside as it would attract bears. That wasn't the way we wanted to see one.

We were grateful for the HOA-supplied wood stocked by the front door— fires were welcome and warm.

We kept in touch with Anemone and Francisco back home. They were hanging in there. The kids got sick, but not severely. While Anemone and Francisco definitely had been sick with Covid they were rebounding fairly well. We were trying to figure out the quarantine days— how long before we could safely go back? At mid-week, we decided to return on Friday, the eighth day after we left. We made the Redbox a nightly excursion. After a long working day, we needed that diversion and relaxation as we ate our soup, chili, salad, or sandwich.

I did take some naps and we did take some short walks around Kingswood but primarily we both kept steadily working around the house.

As the week progressed, the plan became concrete. Xanthus and I would return as soon as the quarantine period was over for Anemone and Francisco and then they would leave that afternoon for Vermont. They would take all the items that had arrived and set up the bedrooms for the listing pictures. Hopefully, they would also be able to rest some without the kids. It would be great for them to see our Lemondrop purchase and give their input, opinions, and suggestions. Hopefully, they would return a little healed from the Covid ordeal. This was early in the pandemic, so they had to stay away from work for the prescribed amount of time due to Covid protocol, which was lengthy. Luckily, they did not have any severe symptoms.

The kid's symptoms were not much worse than a normal cold. We were all grateful for that.

We couldn't investigate any of the shops or restaurants in the area but we did take a couple hikes through the community and adjoining forest while we were there— beautiful, peaceful, rejuvenating. I decided I wanted to live in this white room at the top of the house with its curved window; I wanted to wake up to the sun shining through the window from over the mountain forever.

Growing up, I wanted to get to the big city of Chicago or New York to pursue my dancing career. I did, but I ended up back in Kansas. I still dreamed of the city. When I reunited with the city to care for my grandkids, I found the big city didn't have the same draw for me. Now I knew my dream would be to come to this Vermont countryside as often as I could.

There were still pangs of guilt that it was Xanthus and me who made it to the house first and were making decisions on what to keep or throw away. In retrospect, it was great timing and we were probably the best suited for this cleaning leg of the setup. The next layer of throwaways from the wall décor, etc. could be a group decision. There was still plenty to decide.

Working with my son Xanthus was a wonderful opportunity to watch him begin to blossom in this new business. He showed his skills as a dedicated cleaner, with an eye for details often missed by others. His years of working in the high-end restaurant industry had sharpened his focus on viewing diners through the lens of hospitality. This experience caused him to quickly voice and awaken in all of us that being in the STR business, we were foremost in the hospitality business.

When it came time to leave on Friday morning, I admit it was a little hard. I was missing my grandchildren and wanted to get back to them, but these eight days had been an incredible adventure, and it had been a splendid opportunity to share that adventure with Xanthus. It was a vacation from regular life such as I had never had, and it was hard to end it. I had to keep reminding myself that the Lemondrop Lodge was ours. I would be coming back.

13

We're Live

Paula and Xanthus were up at the Lemondrop, Anemone and Francisco were sick in New Jersey, and I was in my apartment in New York when our listing went live on November 11, 2020, at 11:23 am. Pictures? Check (most of them from Adam's listing). Thanks, Adam. Interesting captions? Check. Description? Check. All the amenities checked? Check.

I didn't feel ready, but I did feel a lot of pressure. Our mortgage, through December, was covered with the closing costs, but we were operating on a shoestring. We needed to generate revenue and we needed to do it fast. I figured I'd get the listing up, and then we'd keep working on it, refining it. We'd keep getting ready. Maybe we'd have a few nibbles in the meantime.

11:27 am: A little red one popped up on the top of the screen.

Booking for December 31 - January 3, confirmed.

My first thought was, *oh fuck! I'm not ready.* I never thought we'd get a booking immediately. I was hoping for the rest of the family to double-check my work, maybe discuss the prices. It was all of a sudden very real. We had our first guest.

I'd accidentally done something smart. I'd underpriced our place. I knew I set our nightly price a little low. I'd spent hours researching comparable listings. Watching them. Seeing what booked and for how much. But as I may have mentioned, I just wanted to get our listing live. I didn't expect anyone to book it! I'd set one price. Same price for every day on the calendar: weekdays, weekends, and holidays. We'd just booked New Year's Eve for about a third of what we probably should have gotten.

I was trying to digest what had just happened and figure out how to respond to our first guest when my phone rang. It was Paula and Xanthus. They were giddy with excitement. Moments later, Anemone and Francisco called. They were disappointed that we gave away New Year's Eve for so little. I felt like I'd let everyone down. As I half listened to them, I was frantically raising our prices. I had visions of our entire calendar booking up in the next five minutes for pennies on the dollar.

Here are a few things to keep in mind when you're ready to go live with your listing. A huge element in your potential success lies in courting the Airbnb or Vrbo algorithms. You need to make that algorithm fall in love with you and your property. You need it telling anyone who will listen about your place.

Airbnb wants you to succeed. They make money when you make money. They want new hosts to list on the platform. They want you to have a chance. So, they're gonna do you a solid. For your first month, the algorithm is going to give you a significant boost in the search results. It's going to get your place in front of eyeballs and see what happens. You need to make the most of this. That first month the algorithm is watching. How many people click on your listing? How many pictures do they click on? How long do they stay on your listing? Do they save your listing? Do they share your listing? And most important of all: Do they book your listing? If you don't do well during your first month the algorithm is going to bury you in the search results and it will be very hard to dig your way out.

I stumbled into a great opening strategy. Sure, we probably could have gotten an extra thousand dollars for that booking, but we got our first booking within five minutes of going live. The algorithm's heart was starting to flutter.

Here's something else to keep in mind if you want to be an Airbnb Superhost (and you do) you'll need:

Ten completed bookings or 100 nights and three completed bookings

An average rating of 4.8 stars

A 90 percent response rate

And a less than 1% cancellation

Every three months Airbnb looks back over the past 365 days and if you meet these requirements, *Boom!* You're a Superhost with all the perks that entails. There are a number of perks, but here's the biggie: You get the Superhost badge on your listing. Besides the elegant aesthetic of the little red badge on your page and the bragging rights now available to you at cocktail parties, it gives you a huge leg up in Airbnb searches.

There are a number of filters a potential guest can check when searching for a place to stay. One of the most popular filters—Superhost. The Superhost badge gives a host validity. It gives the potential guest an added confidence that their stay will be a good one. It still boggles my mind that there is a whole industry based on people paying to stay in stranger's houses. Trust is paramount, and the Superhost badge can help imbue you with a healthy measure of trust.

The majority of searches click the Superhost filter, so if you're not a Superhost you're not even going to show up in these searches. Not only that, but Superhost status is going to give you a huge boost with the algorithm that chooses where you'll appear in the search result rankings. You need to be in the top eighteen listings for any given search result. The top ten is better.

Why top eighteen? That's how many listings people see before they have to click to page two. How many screens do you go through when looking for a hotel, flight, product, etc.? Not many, right? Same for me. Same for most people.

If you're on Vrbo too (and you'll want to be, just not quite yet), you'll want to be a Vrbo Premier Host– their identifier of hosting excellence. They also look at your past 365 days every three months to determine your status.

Vrbo is a little more generous when handing out their rating. Maybe because they don't give you a snazzy little badge graphic for your listing. You'll need an average rating of 4.3 stars, a 90 percent acceptance rate, and a less than 5 percent cancellation rate, and five completed bookings.

Wait, you said I want to be on Vrbo, but not quite yet? Why? Good question. Because both platforms are not only going to boost you in your first month, but they're also going to judge you on your performance. There are only a finite number of days that can be booked in a given month, so you don't want to split the valuable first month between the two. Better to save one for later.

We started with Airbnb. Airbnb was founded in 2008, and by 2020, had over 7 million listings in 220 countries and regions worldwide.

Vrbo, on the other hand, was founded in 1995. Vrbo was originally known as Vacation Rental By Owner (see the name Vrbo makes sense now, right?) The company is now part of

Expedia Group. It has 2 million listings in 190 countries around the world.

Even though Vrbo has been around for much longer, Airbnb has done a great job of gobbling up market share. This is reflected in the amount of traffic that each website receives on a monthly basis.

Airbnb.com had nearly 54 million visits in November 2020, while Vrbo.com had just over 27 million. So, I think Airbnb is the ticket to start, but that can be open to debate.

We were up and running with our first booking, but if we were going to make Superhost on our first look back, and I desperately wanted to, we needed ten bookings. We had about seven weeks in which to get them.

No problem, right? We'd gotten our first booking less than ten minutes after going live! Well, maybe not. We got a little greedy. In fairness to us, we'd taken a huge financial risk on this house. None of us had any experience in the short-term rental business, or the hotel or real estate business for that matter. We had devoured our startup capital just to get through closing. We were paid up through December, but if we didn't make some money by then we were going to be in trouble. So, it was really a necessity– maybe a necessity with a dash of greed.

I jacked up our prices. My logic went like this: If we got a booking that quickly our prices must be too low. Seemed logical, and the prices were on the lower side. But we had no reviews, no track record, no advertising, no marketing, and you might remember we were in the middle of a global pandemic. Our next message came in at 11:45, from Megan:

Do you have any pictures of the bathrooms?

This was something of a sore spot. If you remember, Anemone had loved the bathrooms in the Timber Creek property so much, and they were gorgeous. The Lemondrop's bathrooms were fine, but that was it. They were just fine. Three full baths for a three bedroom are nothing to sneeze at but they were only ordinary and a little small. I figured, just say you have three full baths in the listing and let people's imaginations run wild. No need for pictures, right? Wrong.

Even if your bathrooms are run of the mill, people will want to see them. There are lots of ways to make an ordinary bathroom look interesting. Do some top-notch decorating, offer a plethora of amenities or just some unexpected or particularly beautiful ones, or get creative with the photos. That's what we eventually did– a kind of artsy reflection using the sink mirror and a very curated amenity tray.

At the time I just pulled the bathroom pictures from the real estate listing and put them up.

"Hi Megan, I've added pictures of the bathrooms to the listing. They are all three, full bathrooms. Shower and tub in each.

Great water pressure and lots of light. We've had a bunch of interest since we posted the listing this morning, so the algorithms have raised the price a bit, but since you were our first inquiry, if you're interested, we'll let you have it at the original price that you saw. Thanks, and have a lovely evening."

Yeah, I blamed my price raise on the algorithm. The price had just jumped by 60 percent, probably while she was looking at the listing, and I felt like I needed to say something. We were set up for Instant Book so it wasn't necessary, but I sent her a pre-approval for good measure.

We never heard from Megan again.

About an hour went by with me refreshing our inbox page every fifteen seconds or so, then Nathan at 12:11:

"I have a friend who has a place in Kingswood so I know the area reasonably well. However, could you please tell me about the internet and phone connectivity for your place? I am planning to run my business from there but need fast, reliable internet without tight data caps and throttling by the provider. Is the internet >200mbs download, please? And what cell reception is best there? Thanks in advance."

When you open up a short-term rental you are going to be blindsided by things you'd never thought of. For us the internet was one of these.

Xanthus, Anemone, Francisco, and I had spent the last decade in the New York- New Jersey area, where high-speed internet is ubiquitous. Paula had lived in New Jersey for the last four years, and before that in a little town in Kansas where high-speed internet was also commonplace. It never occurred to any of us that this wouldn't be the case anywhere in the lower forty-eight.

"We can't get internet," Francisco said.

He was in charge of setting up the utilities. Gas/propane, no problem. Electricity, no problem. Cable and internet...

"There's no cable or internet available," said Francisco.

How could this be? Sure, the Lemondrop was in somewhat rural Vermont, but it wasn't Antarctica. We were within the West Dover town limits. There were scores of other towns within a twenty-minute drive and a huge ski resort less than a mile away. How could there be no cable or internet available?

I still didn't believe that could be true. There must be a way to get internet. Still, a panic began creeping in. At the time, you could only ski Mount Snow if you lived in Vermont. People were fleeing the cities back in 2020, trying to find someplace to wait out the pandemic. Many of those people were working remotely ,and you need high-speed internet for that. Mount Snow, our clubhouse, and our pool were closed. If we couldn't get fast internet, I wasn't sure we would be able to rent out the Lemondrop at all.

It was true. No cables were going into Kingswood. There were plans for them, but that didn't help us then. It was such a little thing, but it could bankrupt our whole operation before we even got started.

There must be a way. It's the twenty-first century for god's sake and even in the mountains of Vermont, there must be a way to get some Wi-Fi.

On a personal note, it kind of made me happy that there were still places you could go and escape the insidious creep of the internet, but that was just a personal thing. The Lemondrop Lodge needed Wi-Fi, and it needed it badly. Just then that very same internet, by way of a google search, threw us a lifeline: satellite. That was our only option– one satellite company.

We had an ugly dish put up on the roof and started downloading the World Wide Web at a whopping 30 Mbps. That's just a little faster than sending letters via Pony Express, but not only was that the absolute best we could do, it was the best that anyone in the area could do. It would have to do.

Not so for Nathan. Nathan needed at least 200 Mbps to turn the Lemondrop Lodge into his office.

"Hi Nathan, we all have Verizon and the service is great. For internet, we currently have a satellite with a 30 Mbps download speed. I understand if this may be too slow for your needs but if it works, we'd love to host you. Either way, thanks for your interest."

Nathan: "Thanks for the quick reply. That is likely too slow. Good luck and stay well."

Disappointing, absolutely, but we'd still booked a stay and we'd only been live for a couple of hours.

The rest of the day went by. No bookings. No nibbles. The next day went by. Same thing.

I had to get something going. One cut-rate booking wasn't going to cut it. What did we do? We offered friends and family a *deep* discount if they booked before the new year. We wanted to get a little cash flow, and we wanted to get our ten bookings, but even more than that we wanted feedback.

You can plan and plan and be meticulous, scrutinizing every detail of your property before listing it, but you're going to miss something. If you're lucky, it's going to be something small and correctable, but it could be something glaring. Maybe you're a tea drinker and didn't think to provide a coffee maker. You're not living there, so you're not showering there and forget to provide shower curtains. There are thousands of possible pitfalls, and best to bring as many to light as soon as possible– preferably before a guest experiences them and leaves a bad review.

It's invaluable to have some outside feedback and a different, fresh perspective. That's where friends and family come in.

A word of warning: Airbnb and Vrbo take their review integrity very seriously, as well they should. Gaining people's trust is one of the paramount challenges they faced in building this new category of vacation lodging. Who could have imagined people would feel comfortable letting strangers stay in their houses? Who could have imagined people would feel comfortable sleeping in some stranger's houses? One of the main reasons this works is the reviews. Independent verification. Airbnb and Vrbo know this, and they treat the reviews sacrosanct.

If it looks like your reviews are anything but an honest account of a guest's legitimate stay, you'll get flagged. If you're lucky Airbnb or Vrbo will just take down the review. If they deem this a repeat problem, you will get banned from the site. That's game over. If you get kicked off Airbnb or Vrbo, it will be virtually impossible to grow a thriving short-term rental business.

What type of thing raises these flags? Special offers sent to individuals with a deep *deep* discount. Special offers sent to individuals with unusually low nightly minimums. If someone books without a special offer, you're probably safe because that offer is available to anyone, but still, use caution.

We were flagged. We had five guests, consisting of our friends and family, at $100 a night, no cleaning fee, and a one-night minimum. This was in a two-week period. In retrospect, we should have known better.

We weren't trying to pad our reviews. We wanted people's honest opinions because we had so little experience. We also wanted the bookings to help us on our way to becoming a Superhost. But we weren't asking for anything but honest opinions in return for the deals so it never occurred to us that this could be a problem. It wasn't until several months later that we received a notification from Airbnb. Those reviews were being removed. The notice also included a warning that any fake reviews were grounds for removal from the site.

I still think it's very valuable to get some feedback from sympathetic guests at the start. There are a couple of ways to safely do this. You can block off those dates and do it completely outside of the platform. If the guests are close friends or family this is what I would recommend. Just stay completely outside of the system. You can lower your prices for that time period. Your friends and family can book safely. There is a chance that some stranger will book before they do, but then you have a booking—win, win. You can also send a special offer to your friends and family and ask them to tell you their opinion, but not to leave a review on the site. Airbnb and Vrbo don't care if you give your place away for practically nothing. They just don't want fake reviews. This also gives you the protections you receive through the site. This last option is what I use now if I want to let a friend stay at our place for a discount.

We were lucky. We only had the reviews removed. No review is worth getting kicked off the site. Just keep that in mind.

14

What Does the House Need?

We owned the house, the Lemondrop Lodge. Our first booking was on the books. Yet only Paula and Xanthus had seen the house. The two of them had conducted an extensive inventory of what we owned and it was indeed extensive. The house was furnished— fully furnished, complete with everything we needed to start renting it out. What an incredible stroke of luck. Set aside the money for a moment, it would have taken hours, days— weeks for us to shop and find not, only the necessities, but the things that make a place feel like a home.

According to Paula and Xanthus, the walls were filled with paintings and ski signs. They were a little kitschy, but it sounded like we had a wonderful base of decorations. We could just start adding and replacing instead of starting from scratch. The kitchen was bursting at the seams with kitchen accouterments. The closets were filled with towels, and the beds were covered in sheets and blankets. Paula reported that the bedding and towels were pretty dingy and suggested we get some new linens.

No shops were open for browsing, but we live in a virtual age and, from her quarantine sickbed, Anemone hopped on the internet and went to work. I still don't quite know how she did it so cheaply or so quickly, but the design she put together for our bedrooms was amazing.

This is a word I'll come back to a lot: abundance. Have you ever been to a short-term rental and walked into the bathroom only to find one towel? Or opened up the kitchen drawer to find two spoons? Or one pot and one pan? I have. It is astounding how many hosts try to get by with the bare minimum. A little extra money spent providing a wee tad of abundance for your guests will pay dividends in reviews, recommendations, and return guests, not to mention the overall guest experience.

First, new towels. What color are the towels in every hotel you've ever been? White. It's tempting to go for something fun. The towels aren't the place for that. Get white towels. They can be bleached and cleaned, the color doesn't fade when washing, and when it's time to replace some, you won't have any trouble matching the color. Get as many towels as you can. You don't want a guest to ever feel like they've run out of towels. It also gives your guests a sense that you're taking care of them when they see full racks of towels in the bathrooms, folded towels on the bed, and extra towels in the closet. Get nice big fluffy towels, nice hand towels and washcloths. I would have never thought of this, but Anemone got us a black hand towel with the words Makeup embroidered on them for each bathroom. Not only did that save our white towels and pillowcases from the ravages of makeup removal, but a number of our guests have mentioned what a nice touch that was.

Next, Anemone moved her focus to the bedrooms. Bedrooms are one of the first rooms people look at in a listing, and we wanted to update the look of ours. Themes can be tempting, but be careful. Themes can easily descend into the realm of tacky. Here, Anemone had another stroke of genius. We had three bedrooms. What if each was a season? Winter, Spring/Summer, and Fall. Nothing extreme, mostly just a color theme. Our rounded tower bedroom (Paula's favorite) would be our winter room with whites and ice blues. Our master bedroom would be summer with lush greens. And our smaller bedroom would have all the brilliant colors of a New England fall, making even its diminutive size grand. We hoped that this would also be a subtle reminder that we weren't just a ski lodge. Our house could deliver a beautiful vacation during any season. Sheets are the same deal as towels; they must be white. On the foundation of those white sheets, Anemone built a beautiful design of duvets, throw pillows, and colorful runners, each in the seasonal theme of the room. Like I said, I don't know how she did it for so little money or so quickly, but before Paula and Xanthus returned, she had boxes of opulence waiting to be applied to each of our bedrooms.

Everyone likes to get little surprises for free. We placed an amenity tray on the bed in each of our bedrooms– travel-size shampoo, conditioner, body wash, lotion, toothbrushes and toothpaste, a bottle of water, a little bit of candy, two bath towels, two hand towels, two washcloths. Later I'd learn to fold these into animals, but at the start, they were just neatly rolled.

At this early stage, we were buying all the amenities for the bedroom trays from the travel section at Walmart and, as much as I hate to admit it, Amazon. Don't do that. It may seem insignificant, but the little expenditures add up. I'll say it again, you're running a business and you have to keep records. You have to know your expenses. I built out spreadsheets to track our expenses. We had no real budget, just don't spend too much. The toothbrushes were $1.39. Seems pretty inexpensive, but we put two in each tray and a tray in each bedroom. So that's $8.34 per reservation. Still not bad, but we were doing the same thing with toothpaste. $0.99 a tube. Three tubes per stay. And shampoo $1.45 a bottle. Three bottles per stay. And lotion $1.89 a bottle, three bottles a stay. And... etc. etc. etc. We were spending over $50 per stay just on the bedroom amenity trays.

There are certain things that Airbnb considers necessities and requires all hosts to provide— toilet paper, soap, shampoo, conditioner, towels. I've been to short-term rentals where sits a giant, half-used, family-size shampoo and conditioner in the shower. A lot of short-term rentals do this. It's easy. You don't have to replace it very often and it's cheap. It's also tacky.

There's a famous case study taught in business schools: the American Airlines olive study. Back in 1987 if you were sitting in first class on an American Airlines flight, you'd get a salad with your meal, and that salad would contain, among other things, three olives. Robert Crandall, the head of American Airlines at the time, noticed that if they cut one olive from the salad the airline would save $40,000 a year. It's taught as an example of the impact of small changes. This is something you want to keep in mind, but you have to balance it.

The airline industry, along with a lot of other industries, went crazy with this idea and now what's it like to fly on a major airline? It's pretty much a drag. They've cut amenities, added fees, and taken the experience from an event to a chore. You don't want to do that. You want your short-term rental to be an amazing experience. You want people to be surprised and delighted. I believe, and have found, that this delight translates to word-of-mouth advertising (the very best kind) and repeat guests.

How do you find that balance between delighting your guests and not spending an arm and a leg to do so? It starts with tracking. You might think you have a good idea of what you're spending. Believe me, it's a whole different ball game when you see it in black and white.

I made a spreadsheet with a column for each room. I put in everything that we'd have to buy on a regular basis. The amenities of course, but also toilet paper, tissues, cleaning supplies, etc.

Through this, I was able to get a pretty good idea of how much we would be spending on each stay. Too much, it turned out.

How much should we spend? The industry standard among the better hosts, is 10 percent of the booking price. So if you're charging $300 a night and someone books two nights, you should be spending no more than $60 on amenities.

Seems like quite a bit, doesn't it? It all adds up fast. We've talked about the bedroom amenities and the bathroom necessities. How about the kitchen? One thing short-term rentals have over most hotel rooms: a kitchen. It's a pain in the arse to start cooking a meal only to realize you don't have something you need. Your guests are going to forget the staples when they go shopping because they're used to having them in their own house. Now, I'm not saying you should provide a fully stocked pantry, but there are some things you can provide without too much expense: salt and pepper, ketchup and mustard, butter, olive oil, coffee, tea, sugar, and creamer. Microwave popcorn is cheap and nice to have on hand. We keep a few packs of ramen noodles in the cabinet. This is a prime example of what you're looking for. They're inexpensive. They don't go bad. They fill out the cabinets and add to the look of abundance you're going for. And, bonus, people don't eat them very often so you don't have to replace them every time. If someone shows up starving late at night or forgets to go shopping and comes home from the slopes exhausted, it's amazing to find something to eat in the cupboards. At the beginning, we were also filling the cupboards with individual cereal boxes.

By the time Paula and Xanthus returned Anemone and Francisco had traversed their time with Covid and were feeling well. At this point in the pandemic, no one knew how long people were contagious. The CDC's recommendation of ten days was over. Still, it didn't seem like a bad idea to keep a little distance for a while longer. Besides, the weekend was coming, and Anemone and Francisco had a few more days off. They would be the next of us to see the house. Their trip was brief but valuable. Anemone decked out all of the bedrooms with her new themes. She put together our amenity baskets and a welcome basket and then took more pictures of it all. Our first booking was approaching like a freight train. It seemed like we were going to be ready. Maybe.

15

My Trip to the Lemondrop

I don't mind telling you I was a little jealous. I'd dreamed of owning a house for so long and put so much time into finding this one, and I was the only one who still hadn't seen it. I really, *really*, wanted to see it. The order made sense though, and how lucky were we? Just when we needed someplace for our family to quarantine and keep safe— that's when our house came through. If you are the sort to believe in good omens (although I am not), that certainly was one. I was very grateful that everyone was able to keep safe. I could wait another few days.

While she was up at the house Anemone sent back pictures of the newly decked-out bedrooms complete with amenity trays. They looked beautiful. I was so proud that I would periodically open up the pictures on my phone and just look, tears brimming in my eyes. She'd also put together a welcome basket for our kitchen counter. Wine, jellies, fruit, syrup, pancake mix... It was amazing. I updated our listing with all of these pictures and watched our views rise. We booked another guest. We now had a Thanksgiving booking along with a couple more December bookings.

Anemone and Francisco returned from Vermont on November 16th. Our first guest would arrive on November 26th. It was finally my turn to see the house. All of the bubbling excitement started to ferment into anxiety. I wanted this so badly–this house, this business. I had finally taken a step toward a new life. The past couple months, and all of the major actions, had been virtual: phone calls and emails to the realtor and banks, online research about the market, and online shopping. Even the money was only numbers on screens flying from one account to another. The whole thing didn't feel real to me. Not yet. There was no substance, nothing that was manifest in the real world. That was all about to change. The house was about to become very real for me. What would I feel when I saw it with my own eyes? Pictures can be deceptive. I was very afraid of disappointment. There was no turning back now. My heart raced all the way out to New Jersey.

My heart continued to race at my sister's house, the nerves now morphing into excitement as we loaded Poppy. We loaded up a new set of cheap faux copper cooking pots (don't buy these, they look cool, but they're shite), a mountain of new towels, a set of dishes from IKEA— open stock, so we could replace them one at a time as guests broke them. This wouldn't turn out to be a problem. The first year not a single thing was broken. Can you believe that? A water dispenser and several jugs of water. Digital alarm clocks for each of the bedrooms. This turned out to be a mistake too. The clocks were constantly being unplugged, so that every time we went up after a guest, we were greeted with a flashing 12:00. What wasn't a mistake, the charging cords that went with each clock. Whether they had an Android or an Apple, no one would be in want of power in any of our rooms. The little things make a big difference.

All of these items were real. The first parts of our new business that I could see and touch. It was real. Before long, the car was packed and I was off. Just Poppy and me.

The drive from my sister's house to the Lemondrop Lodge is mercifully easy. First, a two-hour straight shot up I-95 to Albany then a sharp right turn and into Vermont. The first leg is boring. New York highway, nothing really to see, but very easy driving. Good for thinking too.

The worry had subsided while I was with my family loading up the car. I expected it to return on the drive. To be honest, I was kind of dreading it. I'll admit anxiety did seep into my thoughts a bit on that drive. Not as much as I'd expected though. I'd put in the due diligence. Sure, it was a big risk, but we were prepared. We were ready. I was ready.

Just before Albany, I made the right turn. First, you have to drive through some pretty depressed little towns in New York. That only lasts for about half an hour, and then... then you're in Vermont. There's a nice big sign welcoming you to Vermont.

That sign isn't really necessary, though. You would know when you pass into Vermont even if you had your eyes closed (please don't drive into Vermont with your eyes closed). You're chugging along, bouncing over potholes and washboard asphalt, and then all of a sudden, the road smooths to glass. It is kind of hilarious. It's also a vivid example of the spoils of Vermont's high tax rate.

I've done this drive into Vermont before, and I've done the drive many times since. Winter, summer, spring, fall, mud season, it is always magical. The road ribbons through the Green Mountains and you'd swear the landscape was CGI-ed in. As I'd found before, my shoulders dropped and my breath came more freely in this land. It may seem a little corny, but driving through these mountains, I felt like I was a part of them now and that felt good. It wasn't long until I was turning onto the Kingswood properties.

I turned in and drove past the sports center, down the winding road to the Lemondrop Lodge. I pulled into the driveway and there it was– my dream. My Business. My house. I picked up my phone to call my family. My first instinct was to share this moment with someone. I put my phone back in my pocket. I've traveled alone a lot. To be honest, I like traveling alone, but sometimes you see something amazing and you look around for someone with whom to share it and the loneliness stings like a wasp. However, when you're alone you experience the world much more deeply, no distractions. You process your thoughts and feelings at your own pace. I would do this alone.

I opened Poppy's door and walked toward the house, the keys heavy in my hand. The anxiety was back and washed over me like a tsunami. The door opened and I stepped into my house. My house. Even now I feel a rush of sunshine through my veins just typing those words.

The door opened, and I was met by a small vestibule, a nice big closet to my left, and French doors ahead. I was going to take this slowly. I would relish each moment. Also, I was scared. I opened the closet and looked inside. It was a closet.

No more stalling. It was time to see our house. I sucked in a lungful of that crisp Vermont air, held it, and opened the French doors.

This is also going to have to be just between you and me because it's a little embarrassing. My knees turned to jelly and I burst into tears.

When you walk into the house you're met by a hallway, a long bench, and a railing. Vaulted ceilings soared with the same majesty as the Sistine Chapel (at least, that's what they looked like to me). I walked toward the railing and looked over. Below—the living room, our kitchen, dining room, and the sliding glass doors to the deck. The tears were flowing freely now. It was beautiful.

All the anxiety flushed away and joy flooded in to fill the void. I drank it in for a few long minutes. Then I pulled out my phone. I had to share this with someone. Paula answered.

"It's beautiful!" I said giggling like a child.

I then started exploring. First, I went down to the living room. That silly TV in the side of the kitchen counter? It was brilliant. When I sat in the living room the TV was situated perfectly at eye level, and since it was embedded in the counter when it wasn't on, it just faded away. That ugly maroon chair—quickly became my favorite piece of furniture too. I felt like a kid on Christmas morning, except instead of opening presents I was inside of the best present ever.

I had been so afraid the place was going to feel small or maybe dingy in person. Photos can be so deceptive, especially real estate photos. Did I mention I'd briefly worked as a real estate agent? I haven't, because while you'd think it would be germane to the business at hand, it wasn't.

Way back in 2009, after the housing crisis, theaters were folding like laundry. I needed some work. A friend got me into a real estate brokerage in New York City. Not some glamorous, selling apartments to the rich and famous kind of deal. It was the underbelly of the real estate world. It was all commission, renting overpriced micro apartments to poor souls just trying to find someplace to live. It could very well be the sleaziest job I've ever had. I got my real estate license and started out going to apartments and trying to take a picture that would make a dive look livable. It was awful.

I only worked there for a few months, and I made virtually no money. Remember how I said selling was easy when you believed in what you were selling? Well, the flip side of that is that selling is next to impossible, at least for me, when you feel like you're trying to dupe someone. There was one thing I did get out of my brief time as a real estate agent: I knew how you could take a deceptive picture of a room. You may be tempted to use some of these tricks yourself when you're putting together your listing. Don't. We'll talk more about this when we talk about listings, but I like to think of it like this: back when I was an actor it was very tempting to have my headshots retouched and airbrushed, get rid of the crow's feet, straighten my nose, smooth out any blemishes. I never did that. At some point, I was going to have to go in front of the casting director in person, and they were going to see what I actually looked like. For a headshot, you want it to look like you on your very best day. Same thing with short-term rental photos. People are going to see your place in person. You don't want their first thought to be, "Wow, it looked better in the listing."

But I digress, all of that is to give context to why I was so afraid that the house wouldn't look as good, or even would look small and dingy, in person.

I needn't have worried. The house was beautifully designed, and built into a hill; it was only two stories but contained four floors. The house was a physical impossibility– bigger on the inside than on the out. We'd bought ourselves a TARDIS.

With its rounded turret, multi-vaulted roof, and lemon meringue color, we already knew the outside had a very unique cool factor. The inside was even better.

As you walk in the front door you are met by a railing. A quick peek over reveals the living room, kitchen, and dining room all open floor plan and flowing below. Look above and the ceiling soars and vaults to a fan lazily turning high above. A walk to the left leads you to the den, complete with big screen TV, foosball table, and I would learn later, a full cabinet of games. A short flight of stairs and you are in the master bedroom; windows on two sides look out into the beautiful Green Mountain forest and vaulted ceiling again soaring to a ceiling fan. As you leave the master bedroom, before climbing another set of stairs, you can look out over a little railed, rounded outcropping down into the living room. It feels very much like the crow's nest in a pirate ship. Up those last set of stairs is another bathroom, the small bedroom, and our winter room. The winter room looks like a princess's tower from a fairy tale; one whole side rounded with windows. The house was amazing. It was better than the pictures, much better.

We had been so lucky. Do you believe in luck? There are certainly a lot of things in life that are beyond your control. I've often felt like I was being punished for something that wasn't my fault or that I just fell ass-backward into an amazing situation.

Both good and bad luck feel real. I don't know, though. I always remember something one of my old dance teachers would say:

"Funny thing about luck. Seems like the harder I work, the luckier I get."

That thought has served me well in life. It can be hard to put in work that doesn't seem to have a clear linear path to success, or sometimes, to anything. I'm going to get a little metaphysical on you here, please indulge me. The law of energy conservation, Newton's first law of thermodynamics; energy can't be destroyed only converted from one form to another. I'm paraphrasing, but that's kind of how I look at things. Put in the work. Create the energy, create the movement. You don't know where it will lead or how it will convert. It felt like we'd just taken a flying leap on the house, but I'd been looking at listings for five years. I'd spent hours tooling around Vermont, and more than that I'd traveled extensively throughout the country and the world. I'd put in hours and hours reading books and prowling the internet for information. So, while it seemed like we got lucky with the house, I set us up for that luck to happen.

It was an amazing couple of days. I wandered around the house, investigating each room. As I've mentioned, if you're in the short-term rental business you're in the service business. During his time as a waiter, one of Xanthus's general managers, at a Michelin-starred restaurant, told him,

"Put yourself in your guests' perspective. Don't imagine their perspective. Actually experience it. Sit down at the tables; feel how it feels. See what they see. Only then can you anticipate and provide excellent service."

Those are wise words and I took them to heart. I lay in each of the beds. I sat in each of the chairs. I cooked in the kitchen and grilled on the grill. I spent my first few days at the Lemondrop trying to get an idea of how it would feel to be a guest at our house. My brain was bursting with ideas, but we had little money and even less time before our first guests. I felt confident that we would provide them with a good experience, maybe even an exceptional experience. I just wished I wasn't alone at the house. I would have loved to share all the feelings, all the excitement with someone. I would have loved for someone to double-check things with me. That's not how it was going to be though, so after double, triple, quadruple checking everything, I locked the front door and placed the keys in the lockbox. I took a few steps back, looked at our house, my house, filled my lungs with a huge helping of that beautiful Vermont air, and started back to New Jersey.

16

Happy Thanksgiving

It's an eerie feeling having a group of strangers stay in your house. It becomes downright surreal when you haven't, won't, ever meet them. This was our baby, our brand-new beautiful house, and I'd just given the keys to a group of French students on holiday. If you're going to join us in the short-term rental world, this is the business you're in, giving maybe the most valuable thing you own over to strangers. How will you mitigate the risk? How will you find peace of mind?

Are you thinking cameras? There are regulations on where you can put them. No cameras in any bathrooms, of course, and no cameras anywhere that might be considered a bedroom. Do you have a pull-out couch in the den? That's a bedroom— no cameras. Do you have an inflatable bed in the living room closet? The living room is a bedroom— no cameras. So, them's the rules, but here's my take. Don't put security cameras anywhere. Go back to putting yourself in your guest's position. Would you feel comfortable if you thought people were watching your private moments while you were on vacation? There has been a lot of pushback on cameras of any kind in short-term rentals over the past few years and you're likely to get some heat if you put them up in your place. Beyond that though, do you really want to watch your guests using your house? Think about it. Do you?

We use a wonderful alternative to monitor the Lemondrop when we're not there. A Minut sensor. It hooks up to Wi-Fi and, through an app on your phone, you can track the temperature, movement, and sound levels. You can set it to send an alarm at certain decibels or degrees. It also tracks Wi-Fi devices and gives you an estimate of how many people are in your place at a given time.

What more could you need to know? If you rent through one of the big sites, your guests will have to put down a security deposit plus you will have damage protection insurance through the platform. I would also suggest you supplement with some private rental insurance as well. Your guest knows you know who they are and that their credit card will be charged for damages. Not only that, if you build a relationship with them through the online communication, I think there's an added motivation for them to take care of your place. The worst we've had is someone leaving the grill cover off the grill. It froze to the deck and we had to replace it. Hard to believe, but that's it. The entire time we've owned the Lemondrop that was the only unreported damage.

The Minut, or something like it, will alert you when (and if) your guests arrive through the motion detector and it will let you know if there's a loud party through the decibel monitor. I think it's the best of both worlds. Your guests get to maintain their privacy and you get to monitor the important information in your house.

But the Minut would come later. That crisp November day when our first guests were set to arrive, I was on pins and needles. We had no way of knowing when or if they'd arrived. I kept anxiously refreshing our Airbnb inbox, each time expecting a disaster. I was afraid they wouldn't be able to get into the house. I was afraid they would hate it. There were a thousand shadowy fears racing around my mind.

Then at 4:22, a message:

"Hey Paula, we just got in - we didn't have any issues - thank you very much."

The Lemondrop Lodge's first guests were on site! (And with no issues). The anxiety flushed away. I realized my biggest worry, or at least my most present worry had been that they wouldn't be able to get in. It was a silly worry— the lockbox was easy to use, and I'd hidden extra keys in two spots outside the house to which I could direct the guests if they did have trouble. There was no real reason to fear that they wouldn't be able to get in, but we can't choose our fears.

The next day at 1:27, we received another message:

"Hi, which trails would you recommend?"

One reason people use platforms like Airbnb and Vrbo is for the personal touch. You should do your best to be an amalgamation of a concierge and a cool best friend who knows all the best spots. There's no substitute for personal experience, but in a pinch, you can look pretty knowledgeable through some simple googling. I knew about the trailhead on the Kingswood property. I searched local hiking blogs and trip advisories and found a few more trails to recommend along with some details about each of them. I was pretty proud of the work. I sounded like I'd been hiking southern Vermont for years.

This encounter spurred us to something that we'd been wanting to do: make a welcome book. Earlier that summer, Anemone and Francisco rented a short-term rental in the Jersey countryside. Since any type of vacation was impossible, this way at least the family could hole up in a different set of walls.

I'd been looking at the short-term rental business for several years and I'd been talking to the rest of the family about it for just as long. Up until then, they just kind of smiled and nodded, but I think this little staycation opened their eyes to the possibilities a short-term rental offered.

That house they rented was cool. It was very large with a pool, basketball court, and a little pond; my niece and I spent a great deal of the stay chasing frogs in that pond.

The house had endless potential, but the hospitality was abysmal.

When we arrived, the place wasn't ready. The people before us had made a mess, and the cleaners hadn't had time to finish. It can be tempting to try to cram in as many bookings as possible. Put some serious thought into the amount of time you actually need in order to do a turnover. Don't set your turn time based on the stars aligning and everything running as smoothly as shit through a goose. If possible, time a turn. Do the turnover moving at a moderate pace, not flying, then double that time. If you or your cleaners arrive on the premises to a disaster, you want a reasonable amount of time to fix the problem before the next guest arrives. A consistent, good guest experience is going to equal more dollars in the end than what you might be able to squeeze out doing breakneck turns.

This host hadn't learned that lesson. We arrived after a several-hour drive only to find the place not ready. It was hot. We were tired and even worse we had my five-year-old niece and four-year-old nephew along. They experienced some intense motion sickness on the way and we all just wanted to check in and relax. No dice.

Things happen that are beyond a host's control. Things are going to happen beyond your control. As a short-term rental host, as in life, what you do have control over is how you respond.

In this situation you could send your guests to lunch, on you. You could knock some money off the reservation, you could give a gift certificate to something fun in the area. You could send an apology fruit basket to the house that night. Our host did none of these things, and while we had a really fun week, we wouldn't rent from him again. The host lost potential repeat customers over the cost of a lunch.

This host was doing what a lot of hosts do, maybe what you hope to do. He'd bought a house in which he hoped one day to retire and was renting it out to cover the mortgage. Nothing wrong with that. Short-term rental is a great way to build equity in a house on someone else's dime. But even if that is your goal, you're still in the hospitality business and you're going to be way more successful if you think of it that way.

The host got a hard fail on check-in and hospitality, but there was one thing we learned from our stay, besides an inflated feeling that we could do better. He provided a welcome book. It was a three-ring binder filled with instructions about the house, emergency numbers, some local attractions, etc. During our stay, Paula poured over that welcome book and had been chomping at the bit to make one of our own ever since.

Airbnb and Vrbo have sections for some of the info you would put in a guidebook and you should absolutely fill those out completely. There are also several online guidebooks you can build. Hostfully is one of my favorites. You can do one book for free, and it's great for people to browse on their phones before or during their trip.

However, nothing, as far as I'm concerned, beats an old-fashioned physical book. You can have one printed up pretty inexpensively. We use Blurb for ours. They're affordable and super easy to set up and use. A physical welcome book offers you all kinds of opportunities. This is an opportunity to show off and reinforce your branding (we've talked some about branding, and we'll talk more later), which will consist of your colors, your fonts, photos or logos, and the general tone of your business.

You should start with a table of contents so that things are easy to find. You'll want to include a section for necessities; grocery stores, laundry/dry cleaning, and so forth. Include an, in case of emergency section with police, fire department, nearest hospital, poison control, etc. Devote a page or two to house rules and general information about the house: where to take the garbage, the WI-FI password, the way you have to jiggle the handle of the toilet, anything particular to your property. Now you get to move on to more fun stuff. People like the personal experience of a short-term rental. They didn't choose to stay with some corporate Goliath; they chose to stay with you. I think a section about you is nice. Nothing too personal. Just a little bit about who you are and maybe why you love the area or your property.

Everyone likes to eat out; include a section of restaurants. Don't go overboard. An overabundance of choice can lead to paralysis— no more than ten. Shoot for six to eight. Make sure you include different price points and different types of food, a vegetarian option if one is available. You should include pictures (you can easily pull these off the internet). You can also get QR codes for each of the restaurants you include from websites like Flowcode.com. This way your guests can just scan the codes and browse the websites on their phones.

Does your property have a seasonal draw? The Lemondrop is at the base of Mount Snow. We're in a snow town, but that's not all there is to do and winter isn't the only time to visit. What is there to do in your area? What are the local attractions? We used this section to entice people to come back and visit at different times of the year. We divide our Things to Do section into summer, fall, winter, and spring. We are less than fifteen minutes from two absolutely beautiful lakes, complete with water sports, boat rentals and just brimming with fish for the anglers. We are also less than ten minutes from two world-class golf courses, nestled in the stunning Green Mountains. Maybe someone comes to ski Mount Snow, but thumbing through the guidebook ends up booking a golf weekend in the off-season. The welcome book is a great advertising tool. Show off your area. Make sure to include high-quality pictures.

Once you've compiled all this, the welcome book is also a great reference for you. I keep ours by my desk so I have answers at the tip of my fingers whenever a guest asks.

We put one book on the coffee table and one in the welcome basket. "What if someone takes one?" you ask. Great! Now they have a full-fledged reminder and advertisement after the stay. Well worth the $5 or so that you'll spend on it.

We started work on our welcome book that afternoon.

17

How Are People Going to Know That You Exist?

Airbnb takes 3 percent of every booking. With Vrbo, it's 5 percent What are you getting for all that money? Well, quite a lot. Vrbo and Airbnb file all your lodging taxes, saving you a huge headache and a significant amount of time. They provide $1,000,000 in liability and damage insurance. They take care of collecting and processing your guests' payments. They host your listing and maintain your calendar along with general website design. That already sounds like a good deal for 3 percent to 5 percent but there's something that's much more important that they offer, name recognition and market share.

Sure, you could make a website. Set up a calendar and booking platform and try to book guests directly. Airbnb charges you 3 percent and your guests 14 percent Maybe that extra 17 percent is enough to make it worthwhile to build a site yourself, deal with the taxes and lodging fees, process the payments, vet the guests, etc. etc. etc.

But here's the problem— no one knows you. Why would anyone trust you? More importantly, how would anyone find you? Airbnb boasts over 150 million users a year with over 1 billion stays. That's a whole lot of name recognition. Airbnb has even become a verb: "Why don't you Airbnb your place?" When people are shopping around for their vacation it's a no-brainer for them to head on over to the Airbnb website, or to a lesser extent the Vrbo website. Those sites are top of mind for travelers, that's invaluable. It's worth way more than 17 percent.

I'm not saying that you shouldn't eventually have your own website and try to book independently. There is value in that approach, and it's something you should explore, but not when you're starting out. Saving the fees is tempting. Trust me, it's not worth the headache; it's not worth the headache you're going to get trying to run it yourself, and certainly not worth the headache you're going to get from smashing your noggin against the market share brick wall the big sites have built. If it's your first short-term rental, or your second or third, do yourself a huge favor: Start by listing it on Airbnb.

If you design and maintain your listing correctly, Airbnb and Vrbo are going to drive potential guests to your place. You could just stop there. A lot of hosts do. If you have a good property in a popular location, and your listing is at least adequate, you are going to get bookings. Will you get all the bookings you need? Maybe. Will you get all the bookings you could? No.

If you bought or have a property that you use exclusively as a short-term rental, why wouldn't you want it as fully booked as possible? As I mentioned before the overall average occupancy rate for Airbnb is 18 percent; 46 percent for full-time listings. A good traditional hotel occupancy rate is between 50 percent and 80 percent.

Personally, I wouldn't be happy with anything less than a 70 percent occupancy rate. Would you? I don't think so. So how are you going to get there? You're going to have to do some marketing of your own.

Where should you start? You are in luck. These days, comprehensive marketing is available to anyone, no matter the size of their business or budget, but I'm going to need you to resist the urge to cringe. That's what I did when I first entered this field. You're going to need to use social media.

Years ago, I created a Facebook profile for myself. That night in bed I tossed and turned, a cold sweat blooming on my brow. It felt like people were staring, watching me. I couldn't sleep. I had to get up in the middle of the night and delete my profile. Silly, I know. Actually, it doesn't really seem all that silly these days. Anyway, I reactivated my profile a couple of weeks later.

Back then, I did it for networking purposes. I'm a pretty private person by nature, but in theater, as in many industries, networking is vital. I never felt particularly comfortable posting about myself. What? You might say, "Weren't you an actor? How can you be uncomfortable in the public eye?" Well, in my experience there are two general types of actors. Those who do it for the accolades and attention, and those who do it because they want to create something– to maybe understand the world and the people in it just a little bit better, maybe to help others to understand the human condition. I'm the second type.

I had the obligatory Facebook, Instagram, Twitter, and YouTube accounts with extremely sporadic posts. I had, at best, a rudimentary understanding of social media, but I did know its potential reach. I also knew that for a new business with a $0 marketing budget, there was no better bang for your buck than social media.

I opened up Lemondrop Lodge Instagram and Facebook accounts. If you'd like some visuals to go along with this story head on over to one of the social platforms and check out @lemondroplodge. Don't forget to like and subscribe :~) I would also open a YouTube and TikTok account, but that would come a little later.

This is where your branding is going to start to really come into focus. We are the Lemondrop Lodge. What does that mean? Who are we catering to? Families? Couples on a romantic getaway? Adventure seekers? What is our target financial demographic? Are we budget or luxury or something in between? Where would most of our guests be coming from? Nearby? Cities? Other countries?

A lot of those questions will be answered by the property itself. The Lemondrop is a three-bedroom condo. Probably not the place for a couple's romantic getaway. Each of those three bedrooms holds a queen-size bed. Even with the pull-out couch, probably not the place for a group of skiers. Families were going to be our bread and butter.

Next, what's your target price level? Are you going for the budget-conscious or the people seeking luxury? Here, we fall somewhere in the middle. The house isn't well set up to be a crash pad. Besides, we were going to have to charge too much to attract the budget hunters. Are we luxury? No, not really. The house is nice, but it isn't slick and modern. If someone is looking for a swanky luxury ski trip, we are not the place.

Once you know your target demographic you can start to build a brand that will appeal to them. You do a lot of that with how you choose to set up and furnish your property, but right now we're talking about marketing. You don't necessarily need a logo, but your place needs a name. You need to be memorable and not only does a name give people something specific that they can remember, it also anthropomorphizes your place and gives it a personality.

Choose carefully. Once you've narrowed it down to a few ideas, do a google search on each of the names. Ideally, you want to be able to own the name, i.e. purchase the domain. That's hard these days. The internet is a crowded place. If you can't own your domain name you want to at least be able to be in the top ten search results. You'll be able to build a presence and establish your name, but if you choose something like the Cokeacola Cottage people will never find you. (You're also going to get sued for trademark infringement on that one.) If you google the Lemondrop Lodge the whole first page of results, at the very least, are all going to be us. Confusion is a killer in the marketing game. You want people to be able to easily find you and easily recognize that it is you.

Now you've got a target demographic and a name. What next? Establish a tone that you will use in your marketing, one that you will also use when communicating with guests. Are you folksy? Elegant? Friendly? Informative? You want to be able to easily communicate using this tone in an authentic way. Maybe it's just you and your personality. Maybe you want to put on a character.

That's what I did, at least at the start. The Lemondrop was going to be a family business, but one of us would have to be the name on the Airbnb listing. We chose Paula. We had yet to establish our LLC and it made the most sense financially for the account to be in Paula's name.

It had been a whirlwind buying the place and getting it ready. We figured we would all pitch in and get whatever needed to be done, done and so we didn't establish any particular duties for each of us. This was a mistake. If your business is going to consist of more than just yourself, you should have an operating agreement and clearly defined duties before you start.

As I said, we didn't, and since I was posting the listing, I also started doing the communication with the guests. I wrote out our first reply, and when I got to the bottom, I started to sign my name. Then I thought, *It's listed as Paula, I'd better type Paula's name.* Since I was the one learning how the platform worked and maintaining it every day, I was always the one responding to guests. When I wrote to guests it was sort of me, sort of Paula, but more an amalgamation of all of us into the perfect Vermont ski town host. I never lied or really misrepresented myself. I just wrote with the tone of this imaginary character, Paula. It made it so much easier. Maybe that was because I'd spent my life as an actor pretending to be someone else in front of the masses. I don't think so, though. I think it just took the pressure off and let me respond freely without judging or second-guessing myself. Things that I might be embarrassed to say or might think were cheesy flowed easily and naturally. Ironically the imaginary Paula was a lot more authentic than I would have been responding as myself.

I'm not saying you should do this, but I do think that creating a character of sorts frees you up to interact more naturally with guests. It's what anyone in a service or public-facing job does brings forward parts of their personality that are helpful or appropriate for the situation and let other aspects of themselves recede to the background. Communication with guests is so, so important. You should put a little thought into how you would like your guests to feel about their host.

Now you have your target demographic, you have your host persona and tone, so it's time to get down to the nitty-gritty. Choose a color palette and fonts. That may seem a little silly but you're building a cohesive brand. The details and consistency give your brand an identity. This will also save you tons of time later. Since we already used them as an example, let's look at the big soda companies again. That font: You recognize that font without having to read the word Coke. The red: That color is unmistakable to their brand. You could see two soda machines in a strange land and know which is Coke and which is Pepsi just by the colors and fonts. That's the kind of branding you want.

Okay, you have your name, your colors, your brand. Now start posting. The pictures you use for your listing are a good place to start. Posting yourself is great. You know what's even better? Getting other people to post. With each new person who posts or tags you, a whole new group of people is exposed to your property. People you might never have reached on your own. People who are potential guests. Start with your friends. Get them to comment, like, and repost. Friends are a good start, but your guests are pure gold. You want guests to post on their profiles. You want them to rave on their profiles about how great your place is. You want them posting pictures showing how much fun they're having. That's some of the best marketing there is. People are always looking for vacation ideas, weekend getaways, and fun trips and there's nothing you could possibly do that will be more influential than hearing or seeing one of their friends having a blast at your place.

If your place is unique or pretty or fun people might post on their own. You don't want to leave that up to chance though. There are lots of ways to nudge people to post. We were including a bottle of wine in our welcome basket. We made a little laminated tag to hang around the neck of the bottle "Post a picture on Instagram, tag @lemondroplodge, and enjoy this bottle of wine on us." Give people a box of props. In our game room, we have moose antlers, ski goggles, and some silly props. The box says "Make your friends jealous! Post a pic on social media and show them how much fun you're having." On the wall behind we had a friend paint #lemondroplodge in an elegant script. People love taking pictures of their pets. If you allow pets, offer a pet bed, some poop bags, a water and food bowl, maybe a bag of dog biscuits, and a little sign that says something like, "We love our furry guests. Post a picture of your pet, tag @lemondroplodge, and get 10 percent off your next visit." There are so many ways to nudge people to post on your behalf. You probably are having some great ideas of your own right now.

That Thanksgiving, as we sat in my sister's house eating her culinary creations and chattering about what our first guests might be doing in our house, I pulled out my phone to put up a Happy Thanksgiving from The Lemondrop Lodge post.

There was a message. Someone had tagged us. It was a picture of a group of friends gathered around a table, our table, toasting the camera. The picture was captioned, "Having a wonderful Thanksgiving dinner at the Lemondrop Lodge."

I'm something of an introvert myself. I never throw parties at my place. This is going to sound weird, but that dinner they were enjoying was probably my favorite Thanksgiving to date. It made me so happy to see them enjoying themselves in the place I'd provided. It was a beautiful thing to share the house, something that meant so much to me, with a group of strangers and see how happy it was making them. Yeah, if you have, or are contemplating, a short-term rental money is probably first and foremost in your mind. It was in mine. But there are other rewards to renting out your property, meaningful rewards that will stay with you much longer than the money you earn from a stay.

18

Our First Turnover

Are you a planner or a fly by the seat of your pantser? I am, by nature, a planner. I like to attempt to figure out every possible scenario and then come up with a plan. Scratch that. I don't like to do this; I feel compelled to do this. There are some definite benefits to this kind of approach to life. You're usually very prepared and you don't get blindsided all that often. Not all that often, but it does happen. Any given situation is a little like chess. You figure out a plan and the possible repercussions of your move, then make the move. If you're a good player you also think about the possible ways your opponent might respond and how you will counter. If you're a great player you think maybe three or four moves ahead. Chess grandmasters can only think three to five moves into the future. The very best in the world can only think three to five moves into the future, and that's with only thirty-two pieces, sixty-three squares, and one opponent. If you're a planner like me, how do you think you'll fare against infinite opponents making infinite moves in a world of infinite possibilities?

That's the major problem with being a planner: You often become paralyzed by the possibilities. I'm not sure how this trait became so integrated into my psyche. No one in my family is a planner. They're all pantsers, jump-in-and-figure-it-out-as-you-go-ers. Maybe my planning is a reaction to my family. Over the years, I've developed the ability to say, "Screw it" and just jump. I've usually already thought the situation through and am pretty prepared for whatever might happen. I found that this was really hard to do with something as big as buying a house and starting a business. This is one of those places where my family and I made an excellent team. I'd been thinking and researching the idea and the specific market for five years. However, I would have never been able to just close my eyes and jump on my own.

One major potential problem was the fact that we all lived three and a half hours away. Here again, the HOA came to our rescue. Someone manned the front desk at the clubhouse every day. There was a $50 charge for them to go to our house, but we could call them in an emergency. They could also let in any workman we might need to hire. Anything outside? We don't have to worry about it. If there's a big snowstorm, the driveway gets shoveled. If a tree branch falls and breaks a window, a repairman comes and fixes it. Mowing, landscaping, house painting, roof repair, all of it, it's taken care of automatically. If you're going to be living a distance from your property you should definitely take these things into consideration.

One thing we didn't have a plan for was cleaning and turnovers. Xanthus and I were still on furlough and honestly, we wanted to spend as much time up there at the house as possible, so we were going to do the turnovers to start, but was that sustainable? Could we find other cleaners? How much would that cost? Could we trust them to clean to our standards? Those worries swirled around my brain, but for now, Xanthus and I would go up and do the very first turnover for the Lemondrop Lodge.

My sister is three years younger than me and, whether through chance or circumstances, we were virtually inseparable growing up. We lived in a very small town Where there weren't a lot of other children, but I suspect we would have been close even if there were a plethora of playmates available. We spent our childhood days playing, exploring, and learning together. Later in life people often assumed we were twins, which is understandable. We looked very much alike and after spending so much time together as kids, we sounded a lot alike too. We'd spent a few years apart in my teen years, but we re-connected by hurtling ourselves into a whole new world. When I was twenty and she was seventeen we packed up two carry-on suitcases and clutching our one-way tickets boarded a plane to New York City. We were a story out of an old-timey movie— a couple of crazy kids leaving the farm and seeking their fame and fortune in the Big Apple. It seems a little cliche, but that's what we were. We moved to New York to pursue a life on the stage. That's a hard life. Honestly, I don't know if I would have made it if I hadn't had my sister with me. Those early years in New York brought us even closer. She now has a family and a life of her own, but a great deal of who I am today was formed alongside my sister.

My brother is a different story. He's seven years younger. I remember being so excited when he was born. I was going to have a brother to play with too! I didn't realize that a seven-year-old and a baby do not make the best playmates. I kept waiting for him to grow up enough so that we could play together, but a funny thing happened. I kept growing up too and that seven-year distance continued to loom large. I moved away when I was sixteen. He was only nine. So I never spent the time with my brother that I did with my sister. Years later, he also moved up to New York. We spent time together, but we had very different lives, and if you've ever lived in New York, you know how the City can devour your time, leaving little left for forming connections. I was excited to get to know my brother as a man. I was excited to be in this together. I was thinking about all of this as we drove up to Vermont to do our very first turnover.

We chatted about the business and life as Poppy ate up the miles. This was only my second trip to the Lemondrop and it felt like my blood was full of bumblebees. My whole body buzzed as we turned into Kingswood. I was excited. I was nervous too. What would our precious house look like after a weekend of guests? I had visions of holes in the wall and red wine stains on the carpet. There was no reason to think anyone would be punching holes in the wall, but we did give them a bottle of red wine in the welcome basket! What were we thinking? Red wine in the welcome basket?

We pulled into the driveway and walked up to that beautiful yellow house. Our first guests left the Lemondrop immaculate. If we hadn't seen their Instagram post, we might not have even known they were there. We walked through the house looking for disaster. Every room sparkled. They'd even filled out the Covid paperwork we'd left for them on the counter.

Even though the place looked amazing, it was Covid times and we would have to wash, scrub, and disinfect every surface in the house, so we got to work. At the time, Airbnb had an extensive Covid cleaning protocol (40 pages). We'd promised to follow that protocol to the letter in exchange for a cleaning badge on our website and a little peace of mind in our brains.

There are things that you can speed up in the cleaning process, and there are things that you just cannot. Laundry is top of the list of things that don't care how fast you want to go. Wash cycles take a certain number of minutes, and washers only hold a finite amount of laundry. Even more insidious, the law of physics. Water will only evaporate at a certain rate. Towels take forever to dry. This was our first turnover, but I had a pretty good idea that laundry would be the holdup.

First off, I went from room to room gathering towels, linens, duvet covers, and anything that would need to be washed. I would suggest this as a first step for anyone doing a turnover. It allows you to get the laundry started and do a quick inspection of the house for any disasters that may need to be addressed. I would grow to love and despise the laundry. It's a puzzle. There is a most efficient way to do it. I found I liked cracking that code.

We had a stacked washer and dryer in the house, on the very top floor. I stood there and looked at the piles of laundry. One could sort laundry by room, but I decided on type. All the towels together. All the sheets together, duvet covers together, blankets together and so on and so forth.

"What?" you ask, "Duvet covers and blankets have to be washed every time?"

Well, yes. For us, they do. Hold onto your horses and prepare to be skeeved out. Large hotel chains wash duvet covers and blankets when they appear dirty or once every six months, whichever comes first. That's a lot of bodies touching the bedding in between washes. And that's major hotels. Who knows how often or even if most short-term rentals wash their blankets. We could do better. We would do better. Back then during the Covid times, we didn't know just how long or on what surfaces the virus could live. Airbnb's policy was to wash everything. Besides the thought that someone could get sick, could even die because we didn't take the cleaning seriously, that was just unacceptable.

"What about now?" you ask. "Do I still need to wash everything?"

That's up to you. A lot of short-term rental hosts don't. They'll only wash blankets and duvet covers if there's a stain or they start to smell. I'm going to refer you back to Xanthus's number one rule of service: Put yourself in the place of your guest. See the situation through their eyes. How would you feel knowing you were sleeping under blankets that swaddled the bodies of countless strangers with nary a wash? I thought so. Blankets and duvet covers have to be washed every time.

Okay, so now that I knew I was washing everything how best to start? Like anything else, if you don't measure and track the data you're not going to know if you do, or can, improve. I pulled out my notebook and opened the stopwatch on my iPhone. Now prepared to track the progress, how best to start? Wash cycles were going to take the same amount of time no matter what was in the washer. The dryer is where the order was going to matter. What would take the longest to dry?

We had a nice thick, fluffy white blanket for each of the beds. They were going to take forever to dry. Those would go in first. The wash cycle is thirty minutes. In the future, I'd learn to put those thirty minutes to use, but I'm afraid on this first turnover, Xanthus and I spent that time just looking around and exploring.

As soon as the blankets were done with the wash cycle, they went into the dryer and I piled the sheets into the washer. Why the sheets? Why not the towels? Surely, they would take much longer to dry. True, but I was trying to see the big picture. We had complete sets of bedding for each room. Paula had meticulously learned to fold fitted sheets and had found and labeled plastic zipper bags for each item. I could just start making up the rooms with those. But then I'd have to fold all of the freshly washed bedding and re-pack it. I thought it would be quicker to just wash the sheets first and wait to make up the beds. I was right. I then got down to cleaning in earnest. I started with the upstairs bathroom. It was right next to the washer and dryer, so I could keep an eye on the laundry. I also figured bathrooms would be my least favorite cleaning task and I wanted to get that over with first. You may think I'm crazy, but I enjoy cleaning. I love cleaning my own house. I find it's one of the most relaxing things I can do. Clean is pretty much universally accepted as better than dirty, so when you're cleaning, you don't have to question whether what you're doing is worthwhile, or if there's a point to your actions or not. It's also simple and measurable. It doesn't take a lot of brain power to clean, and when you're done you can see the results. In this complex, modern world, a simple task with an easily measurable and noticeable result is a gift. I love cleaning.

By the time I'd finished the first bathroom, the buzz from the washer was sounding, informing me it was time to attend to the laundry. The blankets weren't dry. Of course, they weren't. Thirty minutes isn't nearly enough to dry an overstuffed load of fluffy blankets. I needed to get those sheets dry, though, so I could start making up the bedrooms. We had time. There were a few days until our next guest, but I wanted to see how much time it took to turn over the house. I removed the blankets from the dryer and draped them over our banisters. Good thing there was a lot of available banister space. The linens went into the dryer, and a load of fluffy white towels went into the wash. Here I discovered an unexpected stroke of luck. Mountain air is very dry. That dry Vermont air sucked the water from those draped blankets like a desert explorer at the first oasis.

Xanthus was working on the den, so I moved to the master bathroom. I was already learning. This bathroom went faster, and I was halfway through the third bathroom when the washer buzz beckoned. The sheets were dry, so out they came, and into the dryer went the towels. Next into the washer, the duvet covers. I finished the third bathroom and started making up the beds.

We were spending the night so I left the small room to be made up before we left. That's where I'd sleep. Xanthus insisted he wanted to sleep on the couch in the den. By the time the sheets were on the bed and our fluffy pillows stuffed the pillowcases it was time to attend to the laundry again. If you're following along with the time, you may wonder, "Why did it take thirty minutes to put sheets and pillowcases on two beds?"

It shouldn't. We have two queen beds and a double. I started in the winter room. I tucked the fitted sheet into two corners of the mattress. When I went to do the third corner, the one diagonally across pulled out. I went back to tuck it in, and the opposite corner popped out. It was like something straight out of a vaudevillian comedy routine. I repeated this an embarrassing number of times before realizing I'd grabbed the wrong fitted sheet. In the turnovers to come, this would be the bane of my existence. Somehow, I always grabbed the double sheet and tried to put it on the queen bed. Every time I did it, I thought I'd checked, and every time I was wrong. It was a little consolation that this happened to Xanthus too, until Paula put some bright red stitching around the tag, making it obvious which sheet was in fact the double.

Anyway, the towels weren't dry either, so onto the banisters they went as well, and into the dryer went the duvet covers and another load of miscellaneous into the washer. When the duvet covers were finished drying, the blankets that had been hanging over the banisters for an hour now went back into the dryer to finish drying and fluff and I returned to the vaudeville stage. Even worse than the double sheets were those duvet covers. Over the coming months, I tried many different techniques to wrestle the duvets inside. It was never easy. This first time I found my whole body inside the duvet cover more than once. I filled the calm Vermont air with a string of expletives as I fought with these damnable covers. Even now, years later, it's my absolute least favorite task when doing a turnover. If any of you have a trick for putting on duvet covers, please email us at Ldlkingswood@gmail.com

We continued with the cleaning and laundry. Over time I would keep making tweaks to the laundry order, load size, and hang drying and eventually get the laundry down to eight hours. With one small washer and dryer that's just what it takes.

The turnover was easy. Xanthus and I had no trouble finishing, and we both discovered the joys of cleaning a house that you own. There was still no exploring the town due to Covid, but we had a lovely time chatting and dreaming there in the Lemondrop Lodge.

19

How Long Is a Day?

How long is a day? Seems like a pretty straightforward question with a pretty straightforward answer. Unless it's not.

The major short-term rental platforms are a dichotomy; simultaneously user-friendly and easy to get up and running–while at the same time mind-numbingly complex and obtuse to master. This is great news for us.

Anyone can easily create an account, upload some pictures, write a short description, and check some boxes. Then... Boom! You are in the short-term rental business.

It's in these platform's best interest to make it super easy to get started and thereby get as many houses and apartments and houseboats and tree houses and castles up on their sites as possible. It costs them nothing to let you list your place and if someone happens to book, great, they collect their cut. More properties help them gain market share and ensure that no matter what someone is looking, for or where they're looking the big platforms have something to offer. Besides they have many protocols to boot you if you provide a subpar experience for their customers, your guests.

So why is that good news for us? Low barrier to entry and tons of competition? That sounds like a nightmare of a business, right? Well, this is where that dichotomy that I was talking about comes into play.

It's very easy to get a listing up, but that's only the beginning, the very beginning. At first glance, the owner dashboards of Airbnb or Vrbo seem benign and user-friendly, but trust me they are a labyrinth. Each page and option branches off to other options and pages, which in turn branch to even more options. Some pages and boxes double back on themselves. Some can be found by clicking on a picture, but only when viewing the picture on a particular page. Some open up when you check a particular option. And do the platforms instruct you how to find all the refinements you can add to your listing? They do not. Oh, and did I mention that the sites update, add, and change features periodically without telling you? Yes. Yes, they do.

I hear ya, "So tell me again why this is good news for us?"

Difficult but possible is a beautiful combination in business. It puts the opportunity for success squarely in your hands. Let's face it, most people like easy. They like clear. They don't want to put in effort. They get frustrated. You are not one of those people. I'm not one of those people either. You've already demonstrated your willingness to put in effort by buying this book. Personally, I love it when things take a lot of work because the amount of effort I put in is completely under my control. Not only that, but nobody is going to outwork me (yeah, reader, that's a challenge) This is a theme you're going to see again and again in this book. The recipe for success in the short-term rental business consists of one ingredient– effort. There are lots of garnishes, but only one base ingredient.

If you're willing to put in the effort, you are going to succeed. When I started this whole adventure, I knew nothing about real estate or hospitality or short-term rentals. I had to learn it all. But again, good news! Everything that you need to know or learn is out there and available. You just have to supply the effort.

How far are you willing to go? Here's a little example of a mistake we made in understanding the details of the platform and what we were willing to do to fix our mistake. Buckle up. This may offend the more squeamish readers.

When it comes to booking availability, Airbnb has many options in its settings. First, you need to decide if you want to allow Instant Book or require Request to Book. If you choose Request to Book, you will have the luxury of looking at a potential guest's profile, double checking your calendar, evaluating the number of nights and price, etc., and then, and only then, approving or declining the reservation.

If you select Instant Book, all a potential guest need do is put in their dates, click Book, and.... *Boom!* You are booked; no evaluating the booking in any way. Easy right? Request to Book it is.

No! Wrong. If you select Request to Book, you might as well not be on the platform; 70 percent of Airbnb searches click the Instant Book option on the filter, so you're not even going to show up for those potential guests. But even worse than that? Airbnb wants to make the booking process as easy as possible. They know people don't want to search, find the perfect place, and then wait and see if the owner will deign to rent to them. They bury Request to Book in the search results.

I'm not saying that it's impossible to get the maximum number of bookings with Request to Book, well, yes, I am saying it's impossible to get the maximum number of bookings with Request to Book. If you need another indicator of just how important Instant Book is— its importance is one of the only things that Airbnb spells out clearly and often when talking about their search algorithms.

This was one thing in our listing of which I was certain. We had to offer Instant Book.

Now the pressure is on. You better make sure that your listing is set up correctly; your calendar and prices are up to date because there's no room for error. "Don't I have the option to cancel the booking if something horribly goes wrong, you ask?" Not really. Certainly not if you want to be a Superhost. Not only will Airbnb tank you in the search results (canceling a booking is one of their cardinal sins) you will have to complete 100 more bookings or wait 365 days to become a Superhost. The choice is an illusion: You have to select Instant Book.

Okay, better make sure all of your settings are right. If you are listed on more than one site, make sure any bookings are blocked off on all calendars. You can link your calendars. That works pretty well. However, do you trust these two rival companies to always communicate efficiently with each other? I don't. I only rely on the calendar sync for emergencies. As soon as I get a booking, I go to the other site and block off those dates.

So, we're all set up for Instant Booking. I've set it so that the calendar will block off a day between bookings. Neither Xanthus nor I have jobs at this point, so we figured if we got a booking we could just scoot up and clean in a day and have the place ready to go. Easy peasy.

Our guest checked out at noon on Monday. A lot of people try to do a single-day turn and we might have too if the Lemondrop wasn't so large and we weren't so far away. By leaving a full day between bookings, it allowed us to make sure everything was perfect and gave us the time to deal with any potential problems or emergencies. It also gave us the luxury of offering an early check-in time and a late check-out time.

It was Monday, and we didn't have any bookings that week. Xanthus planned to head up and do the turnover on Tuesday. We had that day buffer, so no one could book until Wednesday, right? Wrong.

The clock struck 11 pm, and I was about to hit the hay when the notification came in.

We had an Instant Booking. Lauran was checking in at two the next day.

What?! How was this possible? I was a bonehead. Details matter. I thought I'd covered every base and had everything set up to run smoothly, but I was thinking a day was twenty-four hours. Airbnb thinks Monday ends at 11:59 pm and Tuesday starts one second after midnight.

We'd just had a guest and we didn't know what shape the house was in. Even more importantly we were three and a half hours away. I was in New York City. If I got on a bus right then, I could probably be at my sister's house by one am. Then hop in Poppy and maybe be at the Lemondrop by 5 or 6 am. If this happened now, that's exactly what I would do, but this was only our third turnover, and I didn't think there was any way I could have the place ready in time.

It was the middle of the night, but this is one of the benefits of not doing it alone. I had help. I called Anemone. I woke her up, of course, but she sprang into action. We agreed we couldn't get the place ready in time. If we canceled, it would be bye-bye Superhost for at least a year. We needed to get Lauren to cancel the booking herself.

We'd been having trouble with the master bedroom toilet. It wasn't always flushing completely. We'd had a plumber in, but the problem wasn't resolved. We thought we'd fixed it, but our last guests had let us know it overflowed a little during their stay. It wasn't that bad mind you, but we were having trouble with it.

I messaged her:

"Lauren, I am so sorry. We are having a plumbing issue and the soonest we can get the plumber to the house is Wed afternoon. We were trying to get it done sooner, but I just forgot to mark this week as unavailable. I'm so, so sorry. Can you please just cancel the reservation?"

If she canceled it would be no harm no foul. Three minutes later, we got another message from her:

"Hi okay, no problem– I can't cancel the reservation on my end without being charged :/. Could you possibly cancel on your end? The app is redirecting me to you. Can't cancel on my end."

Okay, what can we do? A few minutes later, Lauren:

"I'm so sorry to be a pain– we are in a bit of a pickle and need to find somewhere to stay due to issues at our current Airbnb.

Would you be able to cancel the reservation so that I'm not charged the cancellation fee?"

Airbnb gives guests forty-eight hours after booking to cancel a reservation on their end with no penalty. Her canceling should still be the best option. I wrote back:

"I am trying to cancel it out on my end but they're asking me to call in, which I'm trying now but you shouldn't get charged a cancellation fee if you cancel in the forty-eight hours after the reservation."

Damn! Since it was so close Airbnb wasn't going to let her just cancel. It was a feature designed to protect us as the hosts, but right now it was a disaster. Lauren wrote back:

"I think since the reservation is so soon it is saying that I will only receive a $165 refund if I cancel on my end unfortunately :/"

Her canceling wasn't going to be an option. We still weren't ready to give up. I wrote back:

"Okay, Lauren we will go ahead and cancel on our end. You should get a full refund. I apologize for the inconvenience. Have a great trip. Sorry, we couldn't accommodate you."

I went ahead, committed the cardinal sin, and canceled Laurens's reservation. That was it. We now had a cancellation on our record. There was no way to avoid it. But could we get it removed? There is a clause allowing a reservation to be canceled if something happens that makes the property un-stayable. The catch is, it couldn't be our fault, we had to not be able to fix it in time, and it had to be something that would make the property *really* unusable.

The toilet. We had a broken toilet. Was that bad enough? Could we make it sound bad enough?

At this point we had to wake up Paula. The listing was in her name, and they might need some personal verification, like a social security number or something.

We started a chat with a customer service agent. If you're a Superhost, there's a dedicated line for support, which is yet another reason to try your damndest to become a Superhost as soon as possible. We explained to the agent that we understood a day to be twenty-four hours. She confirmed that the day switches at midnight, but she wouldn't cut us any slack. We told her that our toilet was broken and we'd been trying to get a plumber in but hadn't been able to get one yet, it being rural Vermont and all. She asked if we had any other bathrooms. We did.

"Couldn't the guests use them? she asked."

"Yes, but the master bathroom would overflow if anyone tried to flush it."

"Was it overflowing now?" She wanted to know.

Here's where we started to enter the gray area. "Yes," we said. "It was horrible. It was overflowing and there are feces overflowing everywhere."

"Well, that certainly makes the place un-rentable," she confirmed. She would cancel out the reservation for us.

We'd done it! We'd avoided disaster. She only needed a receipt from the plumber when he came and pictures... *No!!!!*

Okay, we could get the plumber receipt, no problem. He was coming the day after tomorrow to fix the toilet. But the pictures?

Here's where it's going to get gross. Was the overflow we were experiencing going to be bad enough? We weren't going to take any chances. I would go up in the morning and do the turnover and deal with some pictures.

The morning arrived. With a couple hours' sleep accumulated, I steeled myself for the long drive ahead. First, I took the bus over the GWB and had a quick palaver with the family. We would stage a photo. I went into my sister's backyard and shoveled some dirt into a little bag. Curses! The dirt had tiny rocks and fertilizer pellets peppered throughout. I started removing them one at a time. When I thought the bag was full enough everyone wished me luck, I hopped in Poppy and started on my way.

Straight up I-95 to Albany and then across to Vermont and it's a magical roller coaster ride through the mountains. I used to think I would get tired of that drive, or at least that it would become mundane. It hasn't, not yet. It still takes my breath away every time.

When I arrived at the Lemondrop, it looked like it'd already been cleaned. We've had amazing luck with our guests. They've always treated the Lemondrop with respect and care. If I'd driven up the night before, I could have gotten the place ready in time for Lauren. As for the master bath, I could have just put a sign on it saying it was broken and that would probably have been fine.

But I didn't. I was armed with towels, dirt, and a camera instead. I reached into the bag and pulled out a handful of dirt. I took a deep breath and into the toilet it went. It looked horrible. This just might work. I wet some old towels in the shower and slopped them around the base of the toilet. Then I sprinkled them liberally with dirt. I wanted it to look right. It needed the right overflow patterns. I filled a pitcher with water and let it spill over the seat of the toilet. It cascaded down, turning the dirt into mud and moving it along with the flow. I added some more dirt. More. It still didn't look quite right. I couldn't bring myself to touch the mess. That must be a good sign, right? I grabbed a pair of rubber gloves and sloshed the towels around a bit, mixing and churning the mess. It was perfect. Perfectly disgusting.

I took the photos. Now I had to clean it up. *Ugh*. I knew it was just mud but it was disgusting. About a half hour later, the bathroom was sparkling clean again. We sent off the picture and the receipt from the plumber, and the case was closed. You don't want to go through something like that. Keep a close eye on your settings and booking windows.

20

First, Do No Harm

I love Vermont. I grew up in a micro-town in Kansas before my family graduated to a slightly larger small town in Kansas. In many ways, it was idyllic. As a child, I was safe and I was free. I roamed and explored to my heart's content. I was free to ride my pony to a little pond, climb a tree, and daydream for hours. The flat landscape stretched to the horizon and provided ample space for my imagination to soar.

However, as I grew older, I longed to escape that small town. I was an unusual little fellow. I was interested in unusual things, and there simply weren't enough people around for me to find ones with whom I'd click. Not only that, but I felt like I was on constant display. I didn't have anything to hide, but my introverted soul longed for anonymity. In that little town, everyone knew everyone. Whenever I went out I had to interact. I remember my first year in New York City. The anonymity left me frolicsome. I could go out, do whatever I wanted, wear whatever I wanted, and not only would no one care, but no one would even notice.

I've spent my adult life in New York City, and until relatively recently, I would have insisted I was a city boy through and through.

Then, a few years back, I started traveling through New England. I was dating a traveling sales rep for a big publisher at the time. I would tag along with her whenever I had the chance. That was pretty often, as it happens, since my job at the Metropolitan Opera afforded me a decadent ten weeks off during the summer. Her trips took us to many little towns and villages in Massachusetts, New Hampshire, Connecticut, Rhode Island, and Vermont.

Of course, I was struck by the beauty of the landscape the trees, the mountains, the rivers... So much more character than the plains I'd known as a child. But what surprised me even more was the people. New Englanders have a reputation for their kind of cold, crusty demeanor, and I suppose at first glance that's what you might see. It's more complicated than that, though. New Englanders, as a general rule, seem to value their privacy and they afford that same privacy to others. While traveling through New England, I never got the feeling that I was a stranger and being watched. It felt like if I let them go about their business, they would do the same for me. It was so different from the Midwest of my youth where everyone wanted to be a part of everyone else's lives.

But it wasn't like New York either, where everyone armored up with an impenetrable shell and a weaponized demeanor when stepping outside. The people in New England, and Vermont in particular, seemed to have a beautiful balance of be and let be and a deep sense of community. It made me feel at home in a way I'd never experienced.

One weekend, we were on our way to see a band in a little town. New England is dotted with little towns, and if you look you can always find something interesting to do within a short drive. Before the show, we stopped by a dive bar that boasted a large selection of beer from local breweries. Walking into the bar, it looked like any of a hundred different bars from back home in Kansas. Perched on bar stools sat two old farmers right out of central casting complete with overalls and John Deere hats. I knew these men. I'd seen them a hundred times growing up. I didn't know these men at all.

A short while later we sat at our table, beer and burgers in front of us. My friend was trying valiantly (and unsuccessfully) to teach me to appreciate beer when the two of them walked in. Two drag queens fully decked out from heels to hair. I suppose I was a little surprised to see them in a dive bar in rural Vermont, but I'd spent twenty years in New York City, drag queens usually don't even register a second glance from me. What did leave me flabbergasted, though, they walked right past the two old farmers and sat at the end of the bar. The fact that they felt comfortable walking into this bar at all was no less amazing than the fact that these two grizzled old farmers seemed completely comfortable for them to walk into this bar. It was a vivid representation of the live-and-let-live attitude that I was learning permeated Vermont.

Instances like that endeared Vermont to me. However, there was a specific moment when I knew I'd fallen in love with the state. I found myself in Montpellier on one of my tagalong sales trips. As usual, I wandered through the town while my friend conducted her meeting. I was about to cross the street when a bright red Mustang convertible pulled up to the stop light. I'm not much of a car guy, but even I could tell that this car was someone's pride and joy. It shined to within an inch of its life; chrome sparkling with a brilliance that threatened to outshine the sun.

I could feel the rumble of the engine in my chest as it idled at that stop light. The man that sat behind the wheel was just as you might expect, an older dude. *Someone's having a midlife crisis.* The thought sprang unbidden to my cynical New York Mind. But just then as my judginess was blooming into a smirky sneer, a woman pushing a baby carriage started across the street. She didn't turn to look at the man in the car. It seemed clear that she didn't know him. Just as she stepped into the intersection, the man leaned out over the car door.

"That is a beautiful baby you have there!"

She looked over at him, smiled, and said without an ounce of irony,

"You look amazing in that car."

She crossed the street and continued on. He drove away.

That was it, but it was beautiful. Two people enjoying what must surely be the respective joys of their lives and taking a moment to notice and acknowledge that joy in someone else. No perfunctory *Hellos*. No small talk after. They both just allowed the other to go back to their day, but I can only imagine, with a little bit brighter outlook. It's corny, I know, but I was moved. I wanted more of this in my life. I wanted to help other people experience this, if only for a weekend or so.

This is important. When you're looking for properties or deciding where to start your short-term rental you need to consider many things. You want to think about what travelers will want and what will draw them to your place. That's not enough, though. You need to love some aspect of it. That's going to show through in every part of your business– the way you write your listing, the pictures you choose, the way you interact with your guests.

I've never considered myself a salesman, yet there have been numerous times in my life when I've found tremendous success selling something. Whenever that happened, it was because I loved something about what I was selling, and I genuinely wanted other people to get that same experience, not because I was adept at tricking people into buying my wares. It's easy to sell when it's something you love.

But with love comes a sense of responsibility. We were still mired in a brutal pandemic. Since the beginning, Vermont had maintained the lowest infection rate in the nation. Sure, part of that was due to the sparse population, but a lot of it was due to the sense of community and personal responsibility that I loved so much. Were we, was I, just some money-grubbing outsider strip-mining the culture I loved?

I was conflicted. We started a business and I wanted to make money. We needed to make money. However, it wasn't all about money. I desperately wanted to have a positive effect on the community. At the very, very least I didn't want to be a net negative.

This all could turn out to be a moot point. Airbnb had not restricted its listings—not yet. Anyone could book, anywhere. You did have to click a little box at booking confirming that you had quarantined and had a negative Covid test. How long would that last? You have to remember how scared people were back in 2020. I was afraid every day that Airbnb itself or the local or national government would shut us down. It wasn't being enforced, but Vermont didn't even want family members from different households going to each other's homes. Me going out to New Jersey to spend time at my sister's house wouldn't be kosher in Vermont.

Would the regulations even matter? What would be our draw? No Mount Snow, no clubhouse or pool or restaurants or antiquing— no nothing. Well, not no nothing. We had a beautiful house in a beautiful state. A state which as I mentioned had the lowest infection rate in the country. People were fleeing the cities in hordes. There was of course no international travel and as we moved closer to a full year of shut down people were going stir crazy. We wouldn't have a problem booking that winter. Vermont was requiring people to fill out a form confirming that they had quarantined for ten days before their trip with all members of their party and had all had a negative Covid test three days before their trip. Even if you have selected Instant Book, you can choose to have a message pop up before someone finalizes their booking. I put a message detailing all of the Covid protocols and informing guests they would be required to sign a form stating that they met all of the requirements when they arrived. I put this in our listing as well. I admit that I was torn. I firmly believe that you can run a successful business while still steering by your moral compass. I also understand that with any business there are bills and expenses that roll in like waves and there are other people to whom you're responsible.

This was certainly the case with our fledgling business. We had our bills taken care of until the first of the year, but that was rapidly approaching. I had put in my cash investment, plus loaned the business another $15,000 to get us through closing. That hadn't been enough so I'd loaned the business another $8,000. I was pretty well tapped out.

Who knew when or if my job would come back or indeed if my industry would come back? I also felt a tremendous weight of responsibility to my family. I hadn't talked any of them into the business, but it had been my idea. I'd been the one who researched and picked the town. I was the one running the listing and marketing. What would happen to them if I couldn't make the Lemondrop earn enough to pay the mortgage? Not just financially either. They were all so excited about the Lemondrop. The thought that I couldn't make it work and they'd lose the beautiful yellow house broke my heart and filled me with dread.

So, I can see how even with the best of intentions a business can make small compromises that eventually compromise the ideals with which they started. I was determined not to let this happen. I loved this place too much. I also valued my self-respect more than turning a profit. I just had to make sure I could keep our doors open, so to speak, during the pandemic.

I was upfront with everyone, both in the listing and with the people I messaged. If they came up to our house, they would have to stay in our house. There wasn't anything else for them in the town; at least at this time. That seemed to be enough. We booked the end of November through December solid and we snagged a two-month booking for January and February.

We closed on the house on November 6th, 2020. By December 1st, 2020, we were profitable. If you'll indulge me a little flash of pride on this matter, I'm really proud of that.

We continued to collect the Covid forms from our guests even though there was no place to send them.

We weren't being shut down. We were getting guests. I could live with what I was doing but I still didn't feel very good about bringing people into Vermont during Covid. Sure, we were following the rules, but were we doing what was right? I hoped that any damage we might do to the community would be slight, and I vowed to bring value to the community whenever I could.

21

It's Snow Globe Time

How do you know when to trust yourself and when to trust the locals? I was in love with Vermont, but I'd never lived in Vermont. Sure, I'd grown up in a small town in the Midwest, but Vermont and the Midwest are worlds apart. If you're going to buy an investment property somewhere that you haven't lived there's going to be a learning curve. One reason people stay at a short-term rental instead of a hotel is for personal insight into the area. You should think of yourself as a sort of concierge/local expert/cool-friend-who-knows-all-the-best-spots. You're not just selling a place to sleep— you're selling an experience.

So how do you become a local expert tout suite? It can be done; it's just going to require a little effort.

First, drive around your area— drive around a lot. You're going to want to do an extensive exploration of the area within fifteen minutes of your place. You'll also want to know about any particularly great points of interest within forty-five minutes, but you can start with the surrounding fifteen minutes. Drive around and write down all of the restaurants, bars, theaters, clubs, and cool-looking businesses.

After you've compiled a list, hit the internet. Do any of these places have a website? I bet they do. Maybe they're on Yelp. Check out the reviews. Make notes, lots of notes. You'll likely want to put together a welcome book but at the very least, these notes will be invaluable when one of your guests asks for recommendations.

Now for a little fun. Eat at the restaurants. See a show at the theaters and do a little shopping in the shops. See what you like and dislike about each of these places. Try to put yourself in your future guests's shoes. What might they like or dislike? Start compiling all these notes into a directory. It's fun to go out with friends and family. It's great to get their perspective on the places too. However, I'm always astounded at how much I learn when I go to a restaurant, coffee shop, or bar by myself. You'll see more. You'll hear more. That information is invaluable. You'll start to learn what the locals know.

That's what I'd do now. We couldn't do that then. Yet again foiled by the virus! No going in restaurants or bars for us. At least not during the first eight months.

One of our major assets at that point was time. With me and Xanthus furloughed, we went up as often as possible. All of the weekends were booked through the first of the year, so we went up mid-week. Turnovers needed to be done, and there were no cleaning people during the pandemic. We did all of the turnovers. It was a necessity and a nice cost saver. That's not why we did it. We just wanted to go up and spend as much time as possible at the Lemondrop. When up in Vermont we would drive around and around trying to get a feel for the area and dreaming about all that would await once the pandemic was over.

The little village was charming, but the landscape was the star. We were smack dab in the middle of a winter wonderland. Little A-frame houses dotted the mountainsides. They looked cool. I'd never seen so many A-frames before. I wondered why they were so common here. Maybe it was something to do with the culture of the European settlers. I thought the A-frames were cool. Still, they couldn't compare to the turreted multi-sloping roof of the Lemondrop.

As we moved into December some of the local restaurants opened for takeout. Every time we would go up, we would order takeout from a new restaurant. It was like an Easter egg hunt, each new order allowed us a peek into the restaurant and a chance to discover a delicious surprise. Just a moment as we walked to the host stand and grabbed our bag of food, it was a glimpse into the community to which we now belonged. It was exciting. It was frustrating. We wanted so badly to learn more about our little town, to experience more. Sure, so we could provide our guests with a better experience, but mostly because we were just so excited about the whole area.

In late December, Xanthus and I were up doing a turnover when it started to snow. The ground had a dusting of snow for several weeks. We'd seen flurries during turnovers before, but this was different. Big beautiful flakes floated down. There wasn't a puff of wind. It felt like being inside a giant snow globe. We both took a break from cleaning and went out onto the porch to watch the snow float down from the sky.

It snows in New York and it certainly snowed back in Kansas. I'd never seen anything like this before. Here tucked away in the mountains, everything so crisp and clean; it was like a fairy tale. I'm not sure how long we watched. We didn't speak. We just drank in the magic. You can't sit and watch snow forever though. We were planning on going back in the morning, and we needed to get to cleaning. Every once in a while, I'd look out the window. Each time, it seemed the snow was coming down faster.

"Hey, come look," Xanthus called from downstairs.

I went down to join him on the front porch. Poppy was gone! In her place a small white mountain. The snow outside rose hip deep and had drifted, completely covering the little orange Prius. There was a *lot* of snow on top of her. I was afraid it would cave in the roof.

"We should at least clear off the roof," I said.

The car sat about fifteen feet from the front door, but it wouldn't be easygoing. We would have to shovel our way to Poppy. Fortunately, along with everything else the previous owners left us a couple of snow shovels. We started shoveling our way out. When we got to the car the snow was still falling. We didn't want to scratch the roof, and there was no way to know where the snow ended and the car started so we started, shoveling and pushing the snow with our hands and a big push broom (also courtesy of the former owner).

We cleared the door, which took another half hour, and went inside. On close inspection, the roof looked fine. I had no idea the structural load capacity of a Prius's roof or the weight of a cubic foot of snow. Looking back at the roof of the house, I began to wonder about that too. I sighed and thought, *This is Vermont; they're no strangers to snow.* They must have built the house to withstand snow. All of those A-frame houses, with the snow sliding off their roofs, now made a lot more sense. We didn't have a garage for Poppy and there's no way we could have dug her out even if we did. We would just have to hope everything would be okay when it stopped snowing.

That night we built a fire in the fireplace, drank bourbon and talked into the wee hours while the snow fell outside. It was heaven.

I'm an early riser, even if the night before had been long and filled with bourbon. I was up at 7:30 and with coffee in hand, I went out onto the front porch to survey the situation. The snow had stopped. The Lemondrop's roof hadn't caved in. Poppy was once again under a mountain of snow, and the Kingswood property was a winter wonderland.

Even as the sun rose. The snowplows were blazing trails. The little road leading down to our place had a black ribbon of asphalt as far as I could see in both directions. The plows were starting to work on the driveways.

A new fear sprang to mind. That plow isn't going to know Poppy is under all that snow! He'll plow right into her.

I wanted to see how she faired the night anyway. It was time to dig Poppy out. This may sound as crazy as back when I told you I enjoy cleaning. I like shoveling snow too. There's something about hard manual labor that makes a soul feel light. I will acknowledge the caveat that I don't have to do hard manual labor every day for a living. Still, out there in the Green Mountains, in my T-shirt and watch cap, shoveling snow felt amazing.

By the time the plowman drove by, he could see the bright orange that I'd unearthed against the white snow. He waived and continued down the hill. I went back inside to make some breakfast. We wouldn't be leaving this morning. We'd gotten twenty-seven inches of snow overnight. Even for Vermont, that was astounding.

Our next guests weren't set to arrive for two more days. I wondered if they'd be able to make it. I needn't have wondered.

This is another example of Vermont's high taxes being put to good use. We never lost power, but there were power crews out that morning for those that did. And the roads, all the major roads were cleared by that afternoon. The side roads took a bit longer, but they too were completely cleared by the next morning when we headed back to New Jersey.

22

Approaching a Cliff

The calendar flipped and we, along with the rest of the world, apprehensively crossed into 2021. The new year didn't bring that sense of new beginnings and hope that she often does. The world was closing in on a full year of pandemic lockdown.

The Metropolitan Opera, my day job, had planned on a January 1st reopen date, but that was laughable. They had canceled the rest of the season back in December. Xanthus had been laid off from his restaurant job permanently. There was no vaccine on the horizon, no plan beyond lockdown and wait it out. What everyone thought would be a week or two break had stretched into a year and now appeared to stretch to eternity. The isolation was devastating and dehumanizing. In New York City, people had started what they called seven o'clock cheers. At 7 pm every day, people would open up their windows and bang pots and pans in appreciation of all the essential workers who were putting their lives on the line to keep the world inching forward. It was such a simple little thing and it only lasted for a couple of minutes, but I found myself looking forward to those couple minutes each day. My psyche drank up that tiny bit of connectedness like a thirsty sponge. The world felt dark and hopeless.

But not so at the Lemondrop Lodge. We'd made it through our first two months. We were making enough money to cover our expenses and starting to chip away at the money I'd loaned the business and our credit card start-up charges. Not only that, starting January 1st, 2021 we became Airbnb Superhosts.

We'd packed in the guests over the last month and a half. Against all odds, our crazy leap of faith– starting a short-term rental business in the middle of a global pandemic– was succeeding. The light from that little yellow house flooded the darkness in my life and filled me with hope. Many people see the short-term rental business as a real estate business— as an investment in property, a way to build equity and generate a little income as well. That's all true, but that's not how I see it. In my view, the short-term rental business is fundamentally a hospitality business. The way I see it, you are providing an experience. Your guests are entrusting you with their money and an even more valuable asset– their time. You are helping them create memories. You are helping them discover something new. You are helping them form new connections with a community and build stronger bonds with friends and family. Your business is the business of enriching your guest's lives. You are building a web of connections with strangers and bringing joy into their lives. This may sound a little corny, but trust me, if you view your short-term rental this way, you will not only stand out from the crowd, you'll also receive a profound sense of fulfillment. That's been my experience anyway.

Xanthus, Paula, and I loved going up and doing turnovers. However, we had done a *lot* of turnovers in the past six weeks. We were also a little concerned about our little Poppy. She got amazing gas mileage and was incredibly dependable, but, maybe not one's first choice for six-foot snow drifts. Vermont kept getting record-breaking snowfall, and while the road crews had been outstanding, we did wonder what January and February might bring.

We could put that worry off for another year because we were about to get a respite. We had one booking for the first week of January and then a thirty-eight-day booking that would take us to the end of February.

Cliff booked way back at the beginning of December. We'd all had mixed feelings about Cliff's booking. Back when he booked, I didn't want to be away from our new place for so long. I was a little afraid of problems popping up. When someone is only staying at your place for a few days, if they're a nightmare you only have to deal with them for a few days. If Cliff turned out to be a problem, we'd have to work with him for over a month. I also felt weird about the money. Cliff was going to pay us $12,000 to stay at the Lemondrop Lodge for five and a half weeks. In the grand scheme of things, that's not that much money. In the future, I'd get us twice that amount for stays of that length. At the time, it seemed like an astronomical amount of money for someone to pay us. I felt very weird about even asking that much for our place and I was concerned we wouldn't be worth it.

In retrospect, those were silly concerns, but they were very real at the time. I'm a worrier, so I'd probably have found something to worry about no matter what happened. However, that reservation did feel like a safety line. Knowing we had a $12,000 payout coming took a huge amount of pressure off my shoulders. We weren't going to have any trouble meeting expenses for a while. It would give me the breathing room to learn more of what I was discovering I needed to know about the short-term rental business. It would also give us a break from the turnovers and Poppy a break from the dangerous roads, which came at a very nice time.

We anxiously awaited Cliff's arrival on January 7th, 2021. Our pool was still closed. Mount Snow was still closed. We did have internet, but it was satellite and while it was the fastest available in the area, it was still pretty slow. Would Cliff be disappointed? I still couldn't wrap my head around someone spending so much money for a vacation rental and I was terrified we would disappoint. Cliff arrived with no fanfare and no email. We wouldn't have even known he was there if it hadn't been for our Minut. It's nice to get a positive message when a guest arrives, but no news is good news. We knew Cliff was there, and apparently, he had no issues with the place. I wanted to expand our social media presence and I wanted to do a deep dive into our Airbnb listing and polish it to a glimmering shine. So far, we were only on Airbnb. I planned to put us on Vrbo as well. As I've mentioned, when your listing is brand new, Airbnb will push it hard to get you bookings and a solid start— same thing with Vrbo. We'd been booking up solid with Airbnb so I was saving Vrbo for when it started to slow. I figured maybe summer; the off-season for our little Vermont ski town. I planned to use this time to learn the Vrbo system and get our listing ready to go.

This is what I was up to, about a week into Cliff's stay when we got his message. No hot water. I'm not gonna lie, I doubt the water was as cold as the chill that ran down my spine. It was mid-January. No hot water was bad, but we had baseboard heat. My limited understanding was that it was powered by hot water pumping through the heat system. Would the Lemondrop Lodge lose heat? We couldn't strand our guest without heat in the middle of a Vermont winter. I called the family. They started to work on figuring out the problem while I looked for other accommodations for our guest. There weren't many options for same-day rentals in the area. I found two. It would cost us a pretty penny, but we could put up Cliff and his family in a place down the road until we fixed our heat issue.

When I called the family, they had updates. Francisco had spoken to Cliff on the phone. Here's a little side note about communicating on Airbnb: They are adamant that you only communicate through their system. Not only do they not provide you with your guest's phone number or email, but they will also X out any phone numbers, emails, or websites that you try to put through their message system.

I understand why. They don't want you contacting guests and booking outside of their system. Still, sometimes it would be nice just to talk to someone on the phone instead of having to go back and forth through messenger. This is one of the few aspects where Vrbo is superior. They give you your guest's phone number and email address. Both systems block out any websites you try to send your guests. This can be particularly annoying when you're trying to give a guest a recommendation or directions. I did discover a little workaround if I want to send a guest a website. I take a screenshot of the website and send that with the address in the browser. Both sites let you send pictures. It's not ideal, but it will work in a pinch.

So how had Francisco spoken to Cliff? He and Anemone found him on Facebook, another boon for social media. It was only the hot water that was a problem; the heat was fine. Thank the short-term rental spirits. Cliff had taken a look at our hot water heater and identified what he thought was the problem. Francisco had called their plumber in Maywood and confirmed a likely issue. It didn't sound like it was a huge problem to fix, but we had to get it done, and quick. No hot water isn't as bad as no heat, but it's still pretty bad. By then it was too late for a plumber, and Cliff was being very cool about the whole thing so we all went to bed and left it for the morning.

Morning came, and Xanthus was right on top of it. He called the plumber we'd found to deal with our leaky toilet.

"Doesn't sound like something a plumber would fix," he said. "Call your propane guy."

Our propane guy was at the property within an hour and diagnosed the problem as a faulty O ring. He had one in the truck and fixed it on the spot. Crisis averted and at a cost of only $250. Not bad at all when you consider the possible outcomes.

We were also super lucky that Cliff didn't throw a fit. He legitimately could have. He was paying a lot of money, and the least he could expect was hot water. This, I think, was a case of us making a little of our own luck. The house was beautifully appointed. There was an overflowing gift basket on the counter and heaping amenity trays in all the bedrooms. We'd taken a great deal of care to make sure Cliff would have everything he'd need and more. That goes a long way. When a guest can see that you clearly care about their stay, they are willing to forgive a lot. It was a little bumpy, but we were off to a good start with Cliff. Now I could focus on some other aspects of the business.

23

Plumping Up Our Listing

Since we had the Lemondrop occupied for a few weeks and didn't have to worry about turnovers or bookings for a bit, I wanted to spend some serious time polishing our Airbnb listing and getting a Vrbo listing up and ready to go.

A lot of people think— just put up some good pictures, check the boxes, write a little description, and Bada Boom Bada Bing, you're all set. That's a start, but it's only a start.

Your first and biggest draw is going to be your pictures. After all, a picture is worth a thousand words, right? There are a couple of schools of thought here. Some people say— don't put up more than eight to ten pictures. You want to show your guests what they need to know in order to book. You want to show off your house, but you don't want to bombard or confuse them. I don't agree with that school of thought. Pictures are a wonderful way to tell a story. Sure, your listing needs to give a potential guest the information they need to make a decision, but more than that, your listing is an opportunity to tell a story. Your listing should help people imagine how they would feel staying at your place. It should help them build a fantasy, a fantasy that you can fulfill. Pictures are an ideal way to build that fantasy. As long as they're ordered correctly, I don't think you can have too many pictures.

The longer someone stays on your listing, the better the chance they will book. You want them to start to feel a connection to your place, so if they don't book, they feel a loss. If Instagram has taught, us anything it's that people will spend time looking at interesting pictures. If people spend more time on your listing, that will also help you out with the algorithm when it comes to ranking. Another bonus: You get to, nay you must, caption your pictures. That's an opportunity to add a whole lot of keywords that will help you with SEO (search engine optimization).

First off, your listing needs a hero picture. That's the picture that people will see in a thumbnail when they're searching. This picture should be the most unique, most eye-catching shot of your property. This is your hook. When people are scrolling through listings this picture needs to make them stop. It needs to be intriguing enough to make them click through to your listing.

Here's a little pro tip: Look at the predominant color for the other hero pictures in your market. Make sure yours is different. Maybe you have a beach house and all the other houses feature beautiful shots of the bright blue ocean. Try to get a picture with a bright red sailboat on that bright blue ocean. Maybe you can have purple beach furniture or an umbrella in yours, anything that will make your potential guests notice you and stop the scroll. The hero picture is all about stopping the scroll.

Our hero picture was a straight shot of the outside of the Lemondrop, with its distinctive rounded tower and unique yellow color. I have a shot of the front of the house in each season and I change the hero picture to match the time of year in which I'm trying to book. Do I get rid of the other seasons? Not on your life. They are great advertisements for the other parts of the year. I just move them down in the listing.

Next, you're going to want to pick your four next best, most interesting, most informative pictures. I do most of our listing editing on my laptop. It's easier with the larger screen and full keyboard, but the majority of potential guests will be looking at your listing on their phones. You must check how the listing looks on a computer and on a phone, extra bonus points if you optimize it for a tablet as well. The information is the same on all of these, but it displays very differently. You need to make sure your listing looks amazing no matter what device people are using.

On desktop versions of the two major platforms, next to the hero picture, they show four more pictures before you have to click through to the picture page. What do you want to put there? Bedrooms? Our Winter room, the bedroom in the tower, looked lovely, and with its rounded bank of windows and ice blue and white color scheme, it was breathtaking. That would be one of the pictures. Our living room has vaulted ceilings, a three-sided fireplace, and a little crow's nest overlook that makes the house look like an adventure— that would be another of our four. The deck looking out into the forest behind the Lemondrop is a great representation of the nature we have to offer. And last but not least, the Olympic-size pool in the sports center.

Originally, we'd planned on hiring a professional photographer, but with a little study, some experimentation, and an iPhone 14, we were able to take some pretty amazing shots ourselves. In addition to the pictures of our house, I pulled pictures from the internet. Make sure not to use any copyrighted pictures. I found pictures of Mount Snow, the lakes, hiking trails, and golf courses— all to give a feel of the place. I put up pictures of a fire in our fireplace with a little tray of marshmallows, graham crackers, and chocolate. I put up a picture of games spread out in our game room. We did close-ups on all of our amenity trays. Then to top it all off, captions for each picture. Captions that enhanced just how our guests might feel when enjoying whatever the picture displayed. Captions like: "Every fall the Green Mountains ignite into a brilliant blaze of color, and the Lemondrop Lodge is the perfect place to experience all the beauty." or "Sometimes wine, s'mores, and a roaring fire is the perfect evening." or "Prepare a gourmet meal in our fully equipped kitchen without feeling left out of the fun thanks to the expansive view from our gourmet kitchen."

By the time I was finished, we had sixty-one captioned pictures.

Wanna see? Hop on over to our listing airbnb.com/h/lemondroplodge and have a look.

If you've got a great set of pictures, you also need a great title and description to go with them. The title is particularly challenging. You'll need to employ all your creativity and economy on the title. Airbnb gives you fifty characters. Vrbo is a little more generous with eighty. Either way, that's not a lot. Some people go with informative: "3br 2bath townhouse close to Mt. Snow large pool." That's forty-eight characters and it gets the information across. Or you could go with something like, "Enjoy a dash of luxury & whimsy 1 mi from Mt. Snow." That's forty-nine characters. Again, the title is a hook. Its only job is to hook enough interest that someone will click through to your listing. Your listing will say how many bedrooms and bathrooms your house has right beneath your pictures. Don't waste your words on that. Tell a potential guest something they can't see in your hero picture. Something that none of the other listings are telling them.

I spent a ridiculous amount of time rolling around words in my mind trying to find the perfect fifty characters.

That's all just the teasers. Then you have to get into the bulk of the listing. You get 500 words to describe your place. Everything I'd read, and it was a lot, said the key was to give the potential guest the information they needed, but also to help them imagine what it would feel like to stay at your place. Few short stories have received as much attention and edits as my 500-word description of the Lemondrop Lodge.

There are a host of possible amenities that take the form of checked boxes in your listing. You want to check as many of these as absolutely possible. Some are immutable. You either have a pool or you don't, but a lot are easy to add, like a hair dryer. It's well worth the $15 it will cost you to pick up a hairdryer to be able to check the box and rank higher with the algorithm. On your listing page, it will highlight the top twelve, but it will also say how many amenities your property offers and display a Show All Amenities button. The Lemondrop boasts seventy-six amenities.

There's a place on your listing where you can post pictures to show the accessibility of your place, such as the width of doors, ramps, etc. Airbnb will verify this. If your property is accessible, you definitely want to highlight that feature. You can also assign pictures to specific rooms, which you'll want to do. It makes them show up in different places.

It's funny; you would think the primary goal of the listing is to sell the potential guest on renting your place. While important, that really is the secondary goal. The primary goal is pleasing the algorithms so Airbnb or Vrbo will show your property to as many people as possible. These two objectives usually don't conflict with each other, but it's an important point to remember. It can be easy to think, *oh, no one will care about that.* Maybe not, but the robots see everything and take everything into account.

You're going to want to spend time on your listing— a lot of time. It can be like a maze. There are options that you can only get to by clicking one specific place. All through the winter months, I kept finding new little sections to add a caption, check a box, or write a little blurb. Like I've said before, this is very time-consuming, but that's good news for us. If you're willing to just put in the time, you're going to rise to the top like an inflatable floatie in the pool. Once you feel confident that you've found and filled out all the little dark corners of your listing are you done?

Nope. Airbnb and Vrbo are always adding to their platforms and they often don't tell you about it. You need to go through your complete listing periodically to make sure you're up to date and nothing is missing; a lesson we would learn the hard way later on.

I continued to refine our listing, prepare our Vrbo listing, and learn as much as I could about the platforms during the slow time of Cliff's stay. When he checked in it seemed like his stay would last forever. It flew by. Before we knew it, it was time to go back to the Lemondrop.

24

Iceberg

Cliff's stay concluded without another incident, and he left us with a plump bank account and another five-star review. We had three days to do the turn before Claudia, our next guest, and her two-week stay. We had easily booked the entire ski season without the benefit of an actual mountain to ski. Restrictions had eased a little. Mount Snow was letting a very limited number of Vermont residents on the mountain. Even more importantly, our sports center was open. That beautiful Olympic-size pool was available to our guests. Again, lots of restrictions, but it was a sign of hope. And if we'd been able to book up without some of our most attractive features, just think what we'd do now that we had a pool, gym, and playroom to offer.

If your property has some natural draw, which it absolutely should, there is likely to be a high and a low season. If you're on the beach, you'll be packed during the summer. If you're at the base of a ski slope, winter is when you'll make your money.

I wasn't willing to resign myself to an empty summer, though. Vermont is gorgeous any time of year. We are a fifteen-minute drive from two beautiful lakes, there are three world class golf courses, hiking, breweries, and mountain biking. I was confident I could entice guests to the Lemondrop any time of year.

Xanthus, Paula, and I talked about all of this as we drove through the winter wonderland that is Vermont. Record snowfall had continued throughout January and February. The landscape looked like it had been painted in. Nothing that gorgeous could possibly exist. But it did and we were a part of it. Again, my compliments to the Vermont road crews. It was easy going all the way to the Lemondrop, even in our little Prius.

I was excited when we finally reached Kingswood. It had been a month and a half. I was completely re-charged, and I desperately missed our little yellow house. I did wonder what it would look like, having such a long-term guest. When we entered, we could barely tell that he'd been there. The place was immaculate. I did marvel at the amount of snow that was now on our roof. It was epic. Everything else in Kingswood was meticulously maintained, so I assumed it was fine. We did a very easy turnover and re-acquainted ourselves with the house. We even were able to go into a couple of new restaurants and pick up our takeout. This town was going to be so cute once it opened. The three days flew by, and soon we were flying back to New Jersey.

~

Claudia's stay was going smoothly. Toward the end of her time at the Lemondrop, I did get a message:

"Some ice fell off the roof and I think it hit some of the deck furniture."

I love Claudia. Claudia is the coolest, most understating person on the planet. I've never actually met her, but I absolutely believe this to be true.

"If it's not in your way don't worry about it," I replied.

This turnover would be just me and Xanthus this time. Just like most of our guests, Claudia left the place in amazing shape. We started the usual routine polishing the place to a glimmering shine. I started in on the laundry. It had become a game: Could I cut a few minutes off the wash/dry time? Was there a different order or technique I could try? Anyway, we were busy and it wasn't until late afternoon that I looked out on the deck.

Holy shit!

Please excuse the language. The iceberg that sank the Titanic had slid off our roof onto our deck. Our steel table— crushed like a pancake under a colossal block of ice. Our grill— splintered into smithereens. Apparently, throughout the winter our roof collected snow. The sun would melt the snow a little during the afternoons, it would compress, and then freeze into ice at night. This was happening on the roof all winter, until a week ago when it warmed up just enough that the ice didn't completely re-freeze, but left a thin film of water underneath. Then gravity ran its course.

It was astounding. I couldn't believe Claudia had been so casual about the level of destruction on the deck. If someone had been out there when it fell... Even now typing that sends a wave of nausea through me. After falling to the deck, the ice continued to melt and freeze. On the deck, a solid floor of ice three feet thick with enormous blocks of ice that had fallen later, jutting from it like Superman's Fortress of Solitude.

We had another guest coming in three days. We had to do something about this. Not only was the deck completely unusable it looked horrendous. If I showed up at a place with that kind of destruction, I'd run for my life screaming.

Xanthus and I climbed atop the iceberg and surveyed the situation. The deck furniture stood frozen solid, locked inside the ice like a wooly mammoth. There was no pulling it out. We tried boiling water, dumping it on the ice, and then sloshing it off the deck with a snow shovel. It was about the equivalent of trying to empty the ocean with a thimble. We needed to break up the ice. I took a few mighty whacks at the ice with the snow shovel. That only resulted in a bent snow shovel. I went out to Poppy, got the tire iron, and attacked the ice with a vengeance. I dislodged enough ice to make a snow cone, maybe. We needed something more serious. It was time for a trip to the hardware store.

I had no idea what we were looking for; I just knew we had to make the deck more presentable for our next guests. We grabbed a bag of ice melt, a big five-pound bag, still I had my doubts. I wanted another option. A hatchet! That's what we needed. Don't get me wrong, I'd probably jump at any excuse to buy a hatchet, but it did seem reasonable. We needed to break up the ice. Besides, a hatchet would be a good thing to have on hand in rural Vermont.

I asked the girl stocking ice melt, "Do you have any hatchets?"

"Are you sure you want a hatchet? You don't want a hatchet," she said and put down the ice melt she had been shelving.

We made our way to the tool aisle, and low and behold! What is better than a hatchet? A great big axe!

I'd used axes growing up, but we'd always just had them. I can't remember ever buying an axe. I figured they'd be expensive. This was a nice big six-pound axe for only $38. It even had a yellow handle to boot. It must be fate. She was right: I didn't want a hatchet; I wanted an axe. They also had a pickaxe, which would have probably been a better choice, but come on— an axe? How cool is that?

Back at the house I donned my knit cap, and a woolen sweater and climbed atop the ice flow inhabiting our deck. I took a few tentative swings and ice chips flew like sparks. After five or six swings a small crack appeared. This might actually work. I renewed my attack with vigor.

It reminded me of the beginning of one of my favorite books: Frankenstein. If you haven't read it, go read it. It's not what you think. The book opens with the crew of a polar expedition chipping ice and pulling a giant sailing ship through the Arctic Sea. When first reading it, I remember being struck by the sheer futility of the action and the unwavering effort of the crews. Which would win out, the ice or the sailors? My little adventure felt no less monumental.

After an hour, I'd been rewarded with some large cracks running through the ice block and a burgeoning sense of accomplishment. Another hour and one large block of ice had turned to many, slightly smaller, large blocks of loose ice that I could heave over the railing of the deck.

There was still ice on the roof. In fact, a sheet of ice jutted eight inches over the edge. I looked up apprehensively every fifteen minutes or so. All I needed was for another sheet to slide off and bury me between two layers of ice. I also worried about when it would eventually fall and how to avoid the same issue I was currently dealing with, but that was a worry for another time.

By late afternoon, I'd shed the sweater and was hacking away in a cap and T-shirt. Huge blocks of ice scattered the ground just over the railing. Some of the blocks were so large it was all we could do for Xanthus and I together to hoist them over. This was going to work. It was a huge job, but it was going to work. After another hour, I'd dislodged our obliterated deck furniture. Xanthus hauled them down to the garbage while I continued to whack. A little while longer and the grill was free. It hadn't taken the brunt of the assault and, while much the worse for wear, was still usable. I chopped until it was too dark to swing an axe safely.

In the morning I was back at it with a cup of coffee sitting on the railing to fuel my whacking. A few hours that morning and our deck was clear. There were several holes where the ice had broken through the oaken boards– another testament to the destructive power of the slide. There was still an overhang of ice on the roof. My first thought was to hack a little of that down, but I decided better of it as I pictured the rest of the ice cascading down on my head. My little knit cap would provide little protection from several hundred pounds of ice. We had done about all that could be done. I made up a little sign on the deck door: Beware of falling ice.

That sign is still up there to this day. Whether it's spring, summer, fall, or winter, we never take down that sign. Xanthus and I made another trip to the hardware store for some caution tape to string around the holes in the deck. The HOA would repair our deck, but not in time for the next guest. There is a certain peace that one feels when you've done a great deal of physical work and knowing there is nothing more that can be done. I worried that our next guest would be upset, but I had done all I could think of, so whatever they thought, that's what it would be.

I did do one more thing. I wrote them a note apologizing for the deck and stuck a gift card along with the note in the gift basket.

"Snow Republic is a wonderful burger joint in town." I wrote "I'm sorry we've had some ice damage on our deck, but if you're in the mood for burgers have a couple here on us. You won't find any better."

Not only did we not receive any complaints from our next guest, but they left us a glowing five-star review. Go the extra mile for your guests. They will forgive a lot.

And what of Claudia? I still couldn't believe she'd reacted so calmly to what, to me, seemed horrendous. Well, not only did she leave a five-star review too, she became a regular at the Lemondrop Lodge.

25

Mud Season

We moved into April, and winter began to loosen her ice grip. The Lemondrop Lodge had been open for business a little over four months. In that time, we'd hosted twelve guests, collected ten five-star reviews, become Airbnb Superhosts, covered all of our bills, and put away a little over $15,000. Things were going better than we could have dreamed. We accomplished all this with Mount Snow, our biggest draw, shut down, our beautiful pool and sports center– shut down, even the state of Vermont— virtually shut down. I felt fantastic. Every day I gained a deeper understanding of the Airbnb platform. I felt confident that our streak would continue.

Why wouldn't it? Now we had our pool. Vermont no longer required paperwork to enter so I no longer had to put a warning on our ad or make people fill out affidavits. There was no knowing how much that hurt us. No one was checking that paperwork and it didn't require any proof. I'm sure some people just signed in. We had been fully booked so it must not have hurt us too much. Still, those restrictions couldn't have helped. At any rate, I had high hopes for the spring.

When we'd started, I insisted we work toward hoarding six months' worth of expenses. I had been so afraid of running out of money. After all, with no experience and the lion's share of my savings used up just to buy the place, it seemed prudent to build in safety nets whenever possible. Also, and I hate to keep harping on this, we were still in a global pandemic, I was still out of work, and there was no end in sight.

Now I think six months of expenses in cash on hand is way more than you need. I think if you can keep three months of expenses, that will be enough to see you through any hitch into which you might run. If you do go more than three months without a single booking, you have bigger problems and likely should re-evaluate your business.

I'd calculated our monthly fixed costs at $3,200. That included our mortgage, HOA, cable, electricity, and propane. These were the costs we'd incur even if the Lemondrop sat empty. It didn't include any amenities, marketing, cleaning fees, or any miscellaneous costs that might arise. I don't include these in the monthly fixed costs because if you don't have any guests, you're not incurring them. I used the fixed monthly costs to determine how much money we'd need to keep the business running if no one rented, and just how much we'd need to have that six-month cushion. If you're doing the math in your head, you know that number is $19,200. We were only about $3,000 away from being able to start distributing profits. Sure, we still had credit card debt, but we had another eight months of 0 percent interest. We were making way more than our costs. I figured as it came closer to the end of 0 percent we'd start paying it off. Any balance left at the end of the promotion, we'd just pay out of our reserves. That would be easy to replenish. Or so thought I.

We crossed into April with a guest and no upcoming reservations. I wasn't too worried. We had money, and surely, I could rope in some more guests. As I mentioned before, when you first list on a platform, that platform will push out your listing for the first couple of weeks. This isn't altruistic. The major platforms know it's hard to book with no reviews, and they want you to book. You booking is the only way they make money. This is true for Airbnb. It's true for Vrbo. I'd been holding Vrbo in reserve for just this situation. Why list your new place on both sites at once? You're bound to waste that push. You can only have one reservation for any given date. Better to milk one platform's new listing push, and then use the other sometime when you need a little help. Now, I needed a little help.

Airbnb is certainly the leader in the short-term rental business, but it may surprise you to hear, Vrbo that has been around longer. I knew a lot of tricks to building a listing from Airbnb and while the Vrbo platform is far from user-friendly, it wasn't too difficult to get the Lemondrop listing up and ready to go on Vrbo.

So there we were with two listings, Covid restrictions easing, pool open and... no bookings.

Our last guest left at the beginning of April. For the first time since about sixty seconds after our listing went live, we had no bookings. I wasn't worried. It was a little slump, but we had lots of money in the bank and this just gave us a chance to spiff up the place after all the winter guests.

We ordered new deck furniture. That cost us about $800. Our lovely deck deserved something nice. We got a new grill. I was super happy we were able to get a great deal on a grill at the local Ace Hardware. I love buying local and they hauled away our old grill for free: bonus. The new grill set us back another $400.

The HOA was in the process of repairing our deck. The damage some of our neighbor's decks had received was cataclysmic. We'd gotten off easy. I thought that since the deck furniture and grill were outside, they would also be part of the HOA insurance, but alas, that was not the case. Still, the deck got fixed at no cost to us; my heart still thumped for our HOA. Speaking of which, our HOA was due every three months. It was due in April. Between our mortgage, HOA, grill, deck furniture, propane... April put a dent in our savings. Still, I wasn't too worried.

In Vermont, April and May are mud season. This year mud season earned its name. All of that beautiful snow began to melt, and the mud flowed. There would be no hiking in April. The restaurants that just started re-opening, closed. It was mud season. Everything shut down. April ended, and still no bookings.

26

Promote

The calendar flipped to May, and we were still bereft of bookings. The United States surpassed 100 million doses of the Covid vaccine. The weather warmed and so did the nation's outlook. Restaurants were re-opening. There were lots of restrictions; social distancing, masks, and proof of vaccine, but I had my first meal out in over a year that May.

While the world was starting to look up, my frustration was rising on the Lemondrop front. I'd spent, literally, hundreds of hours watching YouTube, reading articles, and scouring Airbnb and Vrbo to completely optimize our listing. We were ranking high in search results, but no one was biting. We were getting all the bang for our buck that we were going to get through the platforms. I needed to expand our marketing. But how?

When I needed to learn about business, I'd gone to learn from the best— cover your ears, the name drop is going to be loud—

Harvard Business School. Now that it was time to learn about marketing, where to go?

Several years back, I'd read an article about Google. Google was dissatisfied with the people coming out of universities. They didn't want people who were learning what was cutting edge a few years ago. The world of technology, in particular, was moving too fast for traditional higher education. Google was one of the first major companies to drop their college degree requirements for new hires. They also started their own training program— certificate programs to help people learn what they needed to know now. They offered a lot of programming certificates. Mostly technology-based certificates, but... they also offered a digital marketing certificate.

Well, especially in a time of plague, digital marketing was going to be the ticket. So I applied, got in, and earned a digital marketing certificate from Google.

Mud season was a bust– this year. I wasn't ready to resign us to an empty house two months out of the year. We were building a customer base. Judging by our reviews our guests were having a spectacular time. I thought, *okay they'd come to ski, but maybe we could entice them back during another season.* Our welcome book filled up with beautiful pictures of local golf courses, picturesque lakes, hiking trails, mountain biking, and fall foliage. I added a Things To Do section to the welcome book and divided it into seasons. If someone thumbed through the welcome book during winter, maybe they'd be intrigued by all the fun stuff to do during the rest of the year. We had a brilliant picture of the house during peak fall foliage, a spectacular picture of the house almost buried in snow. During the summer, I'd get a lush green summer picture, blow them all up and frame them. That, along with our season-themed rooms, would help people think of the Lemondrop as an option all year long.

To my chagrin, I'd learned a great deal about social-media marketing in my Google class. We'd had an Instagram account from the beginning, now we also had a Facebook page, YouTube channel, and TikTok account. Try as I might, I just couldn't bring myself to wade into a Twitter.

I started learning video editing and cobbled together little 30-second ads using our pictures and videos as well as stock video and pictures I pulled from the internet. If you feel like you're being bombarded with marketing day and night, you are. But that's in large part because we're living in a wonderful age of egalitarian marketing. Ten years ago, a little 30-second spot would cost thousands of dollars to produce. Now, with an iPad, you can make a professional, engaging ad, complete with special effects, music, voiceover... with an investment of a little time and zero dollars. Even more important than the ease of production is the ease of distribution. Gone are the days when you pay thousands of dollars for a commercial on TV and hope the right people see it. You can put your little ads up on social media for free, and through tags and SEO, get them in front of the right group of people. If you do have a few bucks in your advertising budget, you can pay for targeted ads. Got a place near, say, a beautiful Vermont golf course? Spend $10 and you can get your ad in front of thousands of people who live in the New England area and are specifically interested in golf.

I created an ad for each season showcasing not only the Lemondrop, but all that there was to do in that season, and I started pushing them out through social media, spending a few bucks here and there to test the market.

There are Facebook groups for just about everything. To everyone's surprise, Paula became our Facebook expert, joining and posting on dozens of Facebook groups. Anemone had been making Pinterest boards for ages, so that's where I asked her to focus her marketing time.

As I mentioned before, so much of maximizing your bookings is courting a given platform's algorithm. Every time someone views your property or saves it as a favorite or forwards it to a friend that makes the algorithm happy, and a happy algorithm is going to show your property to more people. So maybe you put up an Instagram post and you got 1,000 views, but no bookings. Was it a waste? No!

First, you're building brand awareness. The more times someone sees your property, the more likely it is to lodge in their brain and if it's lodged in their brain, it's there when they are ready to book. But even more than that, say out of those 1,000 views 5 percent of them click through to your listing. Not to book, just because they're curious. That's fifty views, a pretty high daily number for most markets. And that's from outside of the platform. When you add in the views that you get from organic platform searches the algorithm is going to be giddy and just aching to show your place off to everyone it can.

During these months there was a shift going on inside my brain. I'm not entirely sure I liked it, but I began to be on the constant lookout for ways to move the Lemondrop into the public consciousness. When you start to think like this, you start to see marketing opportunities everywhere.

Winter had been spectacular. Spring had been a bust. We were moving into summer and we had a booking for the end of May.

27

Bon Appetit

Xanthus, Paula, and I eagerly made the journey to Vermont for the turnover after our May booking. It was our first turnover in a while, and the three of us were enjoying ourselves. Like I said before, if you love your property and you get yourself in the right frame of mind, cleaning and maintaining your place is not only satisfying, but it also can be downright fun. Restaurants were open, with masks of course, and we were super excited to start to learn about our little town.

We discovered Dots of Dover, a little diner that would become Paula and Xanthus's go-to breakfast spot. We devoured burgers at Snow Republic, a California-style brewery and burger joint—Xanthus's favorite. A lot of places were still closed, but we were getting a glimpse into just what a cool little town we were now a part of. It was exhilarating. The pandemic couldn't last forever, right? *Right!?* I was excited to keep checking out the local restaurants, but I wasn't the only one with dinner on my mind.

The trash for Kingswood is just a short walk down a hill. Most people drive their trash down, but I usually enjoy taking the walk. I never get tired of walking through Kingswood, and taking out the trash is a nice little excuse. This time Paula wanted some fresh air too, so we grabbed the collected garbage and started down the hill. We yammered away on the five-minute walk down, which is probably a very, *very* good thing. At the bottom of the hill, a short little driveway leads into the woods where a large trash compactor waits behind a metal fence, while a big blue recycling dumpster looks on from across the clearing. I'm always cautious when opening the gate to the trash compactor. Black bears aren't terribly dangerous, but the last thing I wanted was to open the gate and be between a black bear and her freedom. So even though I'd been down to the trash dozens of times, I had my eyes casually to the left looking for movement by the compactor. We were right between the trash compactor and the recycling when I heard a noise. I stopped and looked to my right. That's when his head peeped out one of the doors on the top of the recycling bin.

I stopped dead. "Mom, wait."

That furry face was about eight feet away and staring straight at us.

"Oh my God," I heard Mom say from a step behind me.

I turned quickly to her intending to calmly say, "It's okay."

I'm not sure how calm I sounded, but fortunately, I was loud, because when I turned back, the big furry body was flopping out of the recycling dumpster to the ground. We took two steps backward.

I grew up hiking in Colorado. There are grizzly bears in Colorado, and they are no joke. I knew if we were that close to a grizzly we were probably screwed. Black bears are a different story. They're not inherently aggressive. They are still bears though.

You're not supposed to run from a black bear because you might trigger its chase instinct. You're supposed to make yourself as big and loud as possible, and they will probably just go away. Probably. I'd seen two Vermont black bears while driving and even commented on how goofy they looked. It's a whole different deal when a six-foot-tall, five-hundred-pound wild animal is a few quick paces away.

"What should we do?" Mom asked.

I meant to explain that we were fine, just don't run away. Instead, I think I just said,

"It's okay. It's a black bear."

To my credit, I did say it in a loud confident voice. The bear scampered around the back of the dumpster but instead of putting him farther away, he was now at the edge of the woods, maybe six feet from us. We should have been waving our arms and shouting at him. We did stand our ground and spoke in the loudest, most confident voices we could muster. I was quite proud of Mom. Afterward, she would tell me that it had been a very, *very* long time since she'd felt she was so close to possible death. She didn't panic, though. She just stood next to me and talked while the bear regarded us and then lumbered off into the woods. It was a stroke of luck that Mom decided to walk down with me. I'd become complacent. If I'd been on my own, I likely would have been pretty quiet. Right up until the point when I dumped our recycling on the head of a dining bear and he crashed through me trying to get away. Yes, I was lucky to have Mom with me. You know what else I wish I'd had with me? My phone, or more particularly my camera. I'd purposefully left it at the house thinking I wanted some peace away from it without the constant tug of the device. I do wish I'd been able to take a picture of our new bear friend. Maybe it's for the best though. Some things live much more vividly in our memories without the dilution of photographs.

28

Smooth Sailing?

We'd been profitable in our second month in business. We'd booked our first ski season solid. Our guests were lovely. When we started, I expected to get calls in the middle of the night with problems or show up after a reservation to find the place trashed. That just didn't happen. Now I'm not saying it doesn't happen. I have heard horror stories about guests trashing the place. However, I think you can significantly mitigate that risk by choosing a property that appeals to a certain crowd. Obviously, anyone can rent any property. But the Lemondrop Lodge isn't a party house. It doesn't appeal to a party crowd. We have three bedrooms with queen beds and a pull-out couch, and we're not particularly cheap. We're also cute and quaint. I don't think the Lemondrop would pop out at you if you were looking for a place to party.

There are lots of properties near us that cram bunk beds into the bedrooms. Sure, they can accommodate larger groups, but why? Very few properties add fees for extra guests, and I suspect the ones that do meet heavy resistance on that. More people mean more wear and tear on your place and a significant increase in the risk that it will turn into a party house, not to mention more laundry to do, more dishes required, more toilet paper, etc. etc. etc. Are you going to lose bookings because you don't allow fourteen people in your three bedroom? I don't think so. We have a limit of eight at the Lemondrop, and we've never had any trouble booking up.

We cater primarily to families and families, by and large, are conscientious. One guest accidentally broke a dog biscuit jar. He messaged us, apologized, and asked where he could go to replace it. After being reassured not to give it a second thought he left a $20 bill on the counter after his stay with an apology note. We had one set of guests forget to put the cover back on the grill. It froze to the deck and ripped when we tried to pick it up. That's it. Those are the two damage disasters we had to deal with that first year. Things were looking good.

And then...

Surprise! The Vermont state legislature introduced Bill H25— a ban on short-term rentals. Well, not exactly a ban. The bill sought to institute a residency requirement. The bill would require an owner to live in their house for at least half of the year in order to rent it out. I could feel panic start to tingle through me like electricity. That would mean we could only rent the Lemondrop for six months out of the year. That would put us out of business. We might be able to make our expenses, but a profit would be nearly impossible.

I, of course, knew the perils of regulation in the short-term rental game. My home city, New York, had regulations in place that made it neigh on impossible to do short-term rentals and I'd read many articles about short-term rentals destroying neighborhoods and communities seeking to ban them. This had been one factor in choosing Vermont in the first place. Little ski towns pepper New Jersey and New York too, but New Jersey and New York are lousy with regulations. Vermont isn't exactly "live free or die" like their neighbors New Hampshire, but they're pretty damn close. I thought their "do what you want, just be responsible" attitude would insulate us from any regulations.

Were we going to be shut down six months into this venture? Would we have to sell? Could we sell?

There are lots of problems you can solve, but if your business suddenly becomes illegal, that's a pretty immovable obstacle. I understood this thrust for regulations. Vermont shut down its borders during the pandemic and people still came. Signs stood along the roads at the border: "Please turn back." People still came. Hotels, which are registered and regulated, shut down. People still came. The locals could drive around and see cars with out-of-state license plates parked in driveways– driveways like the one at the Lemondrop Lodge. I felt no little amount of guilt about this myself. Throughout the pandemic, Vermont maintained the lowest infection rates in the country. We were obsessive with cleaning and sterilizing everything between guests. By the time we started hosting guests, Vermont had opened its borders, with restrictions. We required all the needed paperwork and advised our guests of all the local Covid rules and restrictions. You can play the justification game and say that people would have come anyway or that because of all of our precautions, it was safer to stay at the Lemondrop than most other places. However, the fact of the matter is that we facilitated people's trips to Vermont. All that to say, I understood the locals' frustrations.

I also understand how short-term rentals can erode some communities. Wealthy people or companies buy up lots of apartments or houses in a community driving up the prices and gobbling up homes that could be, well, homes. Not only that, short-term rentals can eat away at the culture of a community.

As I mentioned before, it was very important to me that any venture of mine would not only do no damage, but be a boon for the community. I chose our town carefully. It wasn't random and one factor was how short-term rentals would affect the town. West Dover is a ski town. It wouldn't exist but for Mount Snow and the tourists. There are far more ski-gear shops than grocery stores. Every job in the town, at least tangentially, depends on tourism.

Yes, there is a shortage of affordable housing in West Dover, but the Lemondrop wasn't contributing to that. The town consists primarily of extravagant vacation homes. The Lemondrop is in the middle of that range. If we hadn't bought the Lemondrop it wouldn't have been someone's home. It's too expensive. The HOA alone would make it too expensive. It would be too expensive for me to live in. The Lemondrop would have been someone's vacation home. It would have been occupied a few weeks out of the year and empty the rest of the time. Most of the houses in Kingswood were just that– predominantly empty vacation homes. So why is it better for us to run a short-term rental than for someone to have it as a vacation home?

We bring money into the community. I spend a significant amount of time advertising the splendor of West Dover and luring potential vacationers away from any of the hundreds of other vacation towns in New England and along the East Coast. We pay property and income tax and our guests pay lodging taxes on every booked night. Instead of a few weeks out of the year, we have people in the house, spending money in the community, roughly 80 percent of the year. We guide our guests to local businesses where they pour their out-of-state money into the community. We pay local plumbers, electricians, and other workers. Whenever possible, we buy in West Dover— amenities, cleaning supplies, decorations, whatever. I firmly believe that the town is better because of the Lemondrop Lodge. And it's not just my belief, the numbers back me up.

While I did feel some guilt about bringing people into the state during the pandemic, I knew that we were a net positive, and I felt the politicians would know that too.

Still, I wasn't comfortable just crossing my fingers and hoping.

First, I found the state and then local government page and looked up the proposed bills. There was a lot of information flying around out there and, as you may know, with something like this, it's best to go directly to the source. I found the bill. I found the discussion and amendments and I marked my calendar with the date on which the vote would take place.

Next, I looked up our local representative. This is all something you should do before you buy a place. You, for sure, want to know the laws that are already on the books. It's also good to know the tone of the community— maybe anticipate what's coming down the pike. The town in which you choose to buy is going to have a large impact on how much influence you can have in local politics. If you're in a large city, your voice as a small business owner will be all but moot. If, however, you buy in a smaller town you can make your voice matter. I found not only the state government website, but I also looked up our county government website and our township representative.

This is a perfect example of why small market, local governments are so much easier to deal with. Our representative wasn't some career politician with delusions of grandeur; she was the maître d at one of the local restaurants. If you're in a large market and a large town, you're going to be dealing with large corporations and large money. We were dealing with people.

I understood the concern. The short-term rental business is still very new, and as such, it's pretty unregulated. I know there are concerns for safety and that short-term rentals are paying the proper taxes. There are worries that people are coming into communities, buying up properties and sucking money out of said communities. There are concerns that short-term rentals will destroy the culture of a community. There is a concern that short-term rentals will gobble up affordable housing, leaving nowhere locals can afford.

In our area, there was anger from a lot of the local hotels and bed and breakfasts. They are regulated, and they were shut down during the height of the pandemic. Local hotel and motel owners were driving around during the pandemic and seeing cars with out-of-state license plates parked in driveways and were angry about it. Rightfully so. Of course, there were also the large hotel chains that always are up for shutting down competition whenever possible. They would be thrilled to do away with the over 1,000 short-term rentals in the community.

I was confident that in general, and in our community in particular, short-term rentals could be an incredible positive to their communities. I wrote letters. I collected signatures. I joined advocacy groups and tried to amplify other's voices. This is an important point to remember. You are part of your local community, but you are also part of the short-term rental community. It's a community of thousands of people like you, like me and my family, who are running their own little hospitality businesses. You are not an island. What you do with your short-term rental, how you interact with your government official, how you interact with your community and guests, it reflects back on all of us. Be a positive force; that's what I tried to do. Do it because it's the right thing to do. Do it because it makes good business sense. Do it because you will feel amazing.

As the summer wore on and amendments piled up, it became obvious that the bill wouldn't pass. The crisis had been avoided, for now. The thrust switched from a ban to a registry and safety inspections. Which I was all for. I would gladly pay $40 a year to be part of a short-term rental registry. As for safety, our guests' safety is very important to us. We already were following and exceeding the safety rules for hotels and bed and breakfasts. I'd gladly pay a fee to get inspected and get a little safety certificate to display. Partly because I think it's the right thing to do. Partly because it makes good business sense for us. If there is a void of regulation, who knows what might come down the pike to fill it? If there's a registry and safety inspections there's a whole lot less chance that short-term rentals will be outlawed. Besides, and this is probably the theme of the book, other short-term rental hosts aren't going to be willing to work as hard as we are. There are bound to be some people who get shut down because they don't register or because they don't meet safety standards. And I guess the final plus is that it makes the whole industry more above board and legitimate. In my mind, that's a good thing.

29

You Can't Please Everyone, Even When You Do

You can curate your listing to perfection, provide beautiful pictures and descriptions that paint a vivid picture of how one might feel during a stay in your place. You can provide endless facts about your property and the surrounding community, but what's going to give all of that validity? Your reviews. Your reviews give guests confidence when booking. They are one of the five thresholds you must pass to become a Superhost or Premier Host. And maybe most importantly, they are a major element in your algorithmic search result ranking. I'm sure that by now you're beginning to see a pattern. Basically everything we do is in service to either our guests's experiences or our ranking in the search engine algorithms.

How can you maintain a perfect five-star review ranking? You can't. This is going to be hard to hear for some of you perfectionists out there. It certainly was for me. I've lived in the world long enough to know that no matter what you do, no matter how good you are, you're going to eventually run across someone for whom it's just not good enough. Still, I think deep down I thought I could keep our perfect ranking indefinitely.

Our review list was pristine. Twenty-six guests so far and twenty-six five-star reviews across the board. I was very proud of our reviews. Then we moved into late fall, and we met Laura.

We were in the difficult season right between the spectacular fall foliage and the magical winter snow. The landscape is still beautiful, however, it's probably at its least beautiful of the year and people have either just gone on vacation or were eagerly anticipating their winter ski trips. What to do? Let the Lemondrop stay vacant? Nope. We lowered our nightly stay minimum to one night. This is always a tricky call. At least, it is for us. All those amenities and welcome gifts we provide, well the shorter the stay, they become a larger and larger percentage of the rental fee. Maybe most importantly, we were still doing all of our turnovers, along with the seven-hour round trip those included. A one-night stay just didn't seem worth it, usually. We were still in the pandemic and Xanthus and I were still on furlough from our jobs, so time wasn't a problem. I was greedy for occupancy, so I did it. I lowered our minimum night stay to one night.

And soon we received a message from Laura:

"Your house looks lovely, but am I reading the fees correctly? My husband and I plan on staying one night (Nov 6) for our

35th wedding anniversary. One night is $275…and there is a $200 cleaning fee and $70 fee?"

I get it. A $200 cleaning fee seems high, especially if a guest is only staying one night. But you must keep in mind that the Lemondrop consists of three bedrooms, three bathrooms, three levels, a kitchen, a den, and game room, a deck… Every room has to be cleaned, every time, no matter how long the guest stays. All the bedding and towels have to be cleaned every time (we don't know what was used, and we don't make assumptions). And during the pandemic, we were dealing with even more stringent cleaning practices than might be usual.

I explained this. I explained that the $70 fee was a local lodging tax that Airbnb automatically adds, and I pointed out that we were already offering a 46 percent discount on our nightly stay.

Laura wrote back:

"Oh, Okay that's a little out of our budget for one night. Thank you."

I was hungry for occupancy and revenue plus it was only three days before the stay. What were the chances we'd get another booking? Also, she wanted to celebrate her thirty-fifth wedding anniversary at the Lemondrop. I wanted to make that happen for her.

I wrote back:

"I'll knock $100 off the cleaning fee if that would help you. I've sent you a special offer. Either way happy anniversary."

She wrote back: "That's very kind of you. What would the total be? I see the price before fees went from $275 to $350. I'm confused"

I replied: "I also knocked $25 off the nightly price so the $350 is now a $250 plus $100 cleaning fee."

She responded: "Okay, I have to check with my husband. Our total budget is $400 for the stay."

Okay, I figured. I'm already this far in. Let's make this happen for her.

"If you let me know what fees Airbnb is adding for you, I'll make sure the offer comes in under $400."

She responded with the fees, and I adjusted our rate. She was now getting the Lemondrop for just a hair more than what would normally just be our cleaning fee. Between the amenities and the cleaning, we were going to lose money on this stay. But not everything is about money. We were going to help make her thirty-fifth anniversary special and that means something. I felt all warm and gooey inside, and maybe just a wee bit too pleased with myself. I sent her all of the check-in information and closed my computer, feeling good.

Three minutes later... *Ding*. The notification went off on my phone with an Airbnb message.

"Thank you so much. You are so accommodating and I know this will be a very memorable place for us!! Are there any covered bridges nearby? We are coming from New York (eighty-eight miles away). I'm sure we might see some along the way?"

I'm never a fan of questions in the form of statements, but that's just a pet peeve of mine. In for a penny, in for a pound, I thought. Besides it would be good to have a list of covered bridges compiled for future guests. It's important to be knowledgeable about your area, and if it's not the area in which you live, that's gonna take some work.

"You'll pass several covered bridges on your way, but I'll make you a map and point you toward some more later today."

After a couple of hours of online research, I had a list of the eight best covered bridges in southern Vermont, complete with pictures, descriptions, history, and a map.

"Great! Thanks for the info."

Okay, I felt good. It was quite a bit of work, but that would come in handy later. Sure, we were losing a little money, but we were giving a couple a great experience.

On Saturday, we got a message with a picture of a covered bridge and a picture of two burn marks on our carpet by the fireplace. She wanted to make sure we knew about the burn marks and more importantly that she didn't make them. I assured her that they had been there before and not to worry. She checked out with a note saying they had a wonderful time, and I figured that was that.

Then came the review:

"The Lemondrop Lodge was the perfect romantic getaway for our 35th anniversary. This home is equipped with everything you'll need! Host was very accommodating, and made this weekend happen for our budget (Thank you!) We were welcomed by a beautiful basket, with amazing goodies!! We highly recommend this home & look forward to staying again...with our children! The only downside was; the townhouse is 4 levels ...you enter on the second level (main bathroom & game room), kitchen/Living room is downstairs...bedrooms/bathroom is on the 3rd & 4th level. It's a great workout if you don't mind the stairs. *The heated swimming pool closes at 4:30. We were disappointed, we weren't able to use it."

Not too bad, right? Not so fast. She gave us four stars.

four stars!!!

That perfect five-star rating I was so proud of— *gone*. It was not only wonderful for getting future business, but it was also a reflection of the effort we put into the Lemondrop and each guest's stay. I'm not a fool. I knew that eventually, someone was going to find something they didn't like and give us a bad review. But I didn't expect it to go down like this. We lost money on the stay. We'd basically given her the Lemondrop as an anniversary present. Not only that, I'd put in several hours of research to put together a personalized covered bridge tour for her. Why the four stars?

Airbnb's five-star system does give you a little wiggle room. There are six sections on which a guest is asked to rank your property: check-in, cleanliness, accuracy, communication, Location, value. The star ranking that you see for the stay is an average of these scores. You actually can get a five-star review even if one of these categories isn't. We'd once gotten a 4.9 on value, but the rest of the categories on that stay were five so the overall stay was five and we kept our perfect review ranking. What did Laura have a problem with? She gave us four on location and four on value. I don't know what could have been wrong with the location or what we could have done about that. Maybe she was disappointed it wasn't Paris? But value? Those four stars felt like she asked me to carry her bags, tripped me, and then pushed my face in the mud. Just between you and me, I was angry. Very angry. The thing about the star rankings... they never go away. A cancellation? Drops off your record after a year. Response rate? Same deal. It's gone after a year. Your stars and reviews are there forever. Your overall star ranking is an average of all of your reviews, but once you get less than five stars, you will never have a perfect ranking again. Never. That hurt. I wrote a scathing response but fortunately sent it to the rest of the family to read before sending it off to Laura. Anemone talked me down. It was a good review. A glowing review. And not only would Laura likely be horrified to understand what she'd done to us, it would likely ruin the memory of the experience. "Let it go" was Anemone's advice, and she was right. I sent Laura a curt response saying we were happy she enjoyed her stay.

Our ranking was now 4.96 stars. I vowed to get it up to 4.99 someday. That was the best we could now do. It wasn't the end of the world. Really it just hurt my pride, and maybe more importantly, my feelings. Her written review was glowing, and the algorithm wouldn't punish us for having 4.96 instead of five stars.

A few lessons I learned from this experience:

1. If you stack up as many good reviews as possible, they will dilute any less-than-stellar reviews you might get.

2. You are going to get a less-than-stellar review eventually no matter how hard you try.

3. As with most things in life, you only have control over what you do, not how someone else reacts. If you give the guest the absolute best experience you can provide, you can be proud of that no matter what their review says.

I don't have enough data to include this as a lesson, but I'll point it out for what it's worth. We gave Laura an incredible price for her stay and took a hit on the value rating. The only other less-than-perfect star rating? Remember I told you we once got 4.9 stars on value? The Lemondrop usually rents for between $500 and $625 a night We'd given that guest the house for $175 a night. If your prices are too low, you're going to attract bargain hunters. People who are always looking for a bargain are going to always think they could have done a little better. You want to keep your house occupied, but you might want to keep this in mind as well.

Airbnb and Vrbo allow you to respond to your reviews both personally and publicly. This is a wonderful opportunity, don't squander it. The private response is an opportunity to personally address any issues a guest might have had, but maybe even more importantly, it's an opportunity to build and cement a relationship. Repeat guests are valuable. You know what to expect from them. You don't have to worry about them. When a guest books with you, check their profile. The benefits here are twofold. First, this person is staying in your house, you want to know a little something about them. It can be tempting to try to find your guests on social media or even google them. Don't. Not only is this an invasion of their privacy, but the info you get is going to be out of context. It can only lead to speculation and down that road lies madness. Just have a look at their booking profile. How have other hosts rated them?

The second is a little hack that might help you avoid a bad review. Look at the reviews your upcoming guests have given other hosts. If they had a problem with some aspect of one of their previous stays now you know and you can make sure they don't have the same problem at your place.

30

Alexander's Trip to the Lemondrop

I'd been to the Lemondrop by myself. I'd been to the Lemondrop with Xanthus and with Paula. I'd read reviews and seen people's posts on social media, but I'd never experienced someone else experiencing the Lemondrop for the first time.

It was summer and our bookings were a little slower. Travel restrictions had eased up a little, and our sports center and some local restaurants were open. It was finally time for me to have a little vacation at the Lemondrop. Not just myself, though. My partner Arden, and her son, Alexander, were coming too.

I don't mind telling you, I was nervous. Arden is sophisticated. She spends her evenings at the opera and hobnobs with the refined out in the Hamptons. I was afraid that the little house I was so proud of would look hokey or lame to her. In the short-term rental business, as with most things in life, it's important to develop a thick skin and even more important to have confidence in your choices. I felt I'd done that, but as I'm sure you know, confidence can become a fragile thing in the face of the judgment of people close to you. Still, I was proud of the place, and I wanted very much to show it off to her.

Alexander was a different challenge. He was five at the time. It was a long drive for a five-year-old and after that three-and-a-half-hour drive, what would be his reward? A house? What kind of fun is a cottage in the mountains for a five-year-old? I wanted so badly to give him a fun, memorable experience, but could the Lemondrop possibly be that for a five-year-old?

I've never been a kids sort of guy. I never wanted children, but Alexander was a special case. To begin with, we have the same birthday– February 8th. That's only a coincidence. I know that, and I'm not prone to delusions of fate or the metaphysical. However, the human mind loves to latch onto coincidences, and I suppose I'm no different. He also experiences some very similar challenges as me. I have dyslexia. I didn't learn to read until I was almost ten. He has an auditory processing disorder that affects, his language learning in a very similar way as my dyslexia affects, my visual language learning. I understood the frustrations of a mind that works so well in so many areas but just doesn't function the way everyone else's does in one specific area. I understood how when that difficulty of function relates to the way you get information and learn, either by the written word or the spoken, how it can creep into all aspects of your life and development; I understood what that sort of thing can do to you emotionally. Alexander was dealing with many similar challenges that I dealt with as a boy. I love that kid. This may seem kind of silly, but with Alexander, it often feels like I have the opportunity to travel back in time and help the little boy I once was. I guess I just wanted to be, for him, the man I wish I'd had in my life when I was little.

Anyway, I was afraid the drive would be hard and he would be bored when we got to the Lemondrop.

We got a kind of late start. I hoped that he would fall asleep on the drive. He didn't sleep a wink. It wasn't a problem, though. The little tike was obsessed with my phone. I'm not sure why the games were more fun on my little iPhone than they were on his iPad, but apparently, they were. He was glued to my phone the whole way up.

When we finally did pull into the driveway, he had nodded off.

"Hey Skipper." I call him Skipper, partly because he loves boats and ships, and partly because he quite literally skips everywhere. "We're here."

He rubbed his eyes and followed Arden and me into the house. He was still half asleep, but that didn't stop him from completing a full inspection. I followed him as he walked down the stairs, looked around the living room, and then walked back up the stairs to the master bedroom where he hopped on the bed and declared, "This is my room." Then he snuggled under the duvet and fell asleep.

The next morning, I woke early, made a cup of coffee, and went to sit on the deck, stare into the woods, and think. These are some of my very favorite things in the world: early mornings, coffee, and thoughts. I remember as a kid thinking my dad was crazy. He'd get up super early, make some coffee, and then sit in his rocker outside. Why would someone wake up early just to sit and drink coffee? If you didn't have to get up early, why in god's name would you?

Well, as I've gotten older, I've changed my tune. I love those golden hours when everyone is asleep and the world is quiet.

So there I was enjoying the morning when the sliding glass door opened. The little Skipper padded out, climbed up on my lap, gave me a hug, and said,

"I love you. I love the yellow house," and fell back asleep on my lap.

If mornings hadn't been my favorite before, they certainly were now. We sat there together in the peaceful Vermont morning for quite a while. Arden woke a little later and whipped us up a spectacular breakfast. I looked through the window over the little curly head lying against my shoulder and watched her cook. Arden has worked as a professional chef. It made me proud to see her in my kitchen finding everything she needed and enjoying the process. We had bacon, eggs, pancakes, and a host of other delicacies out there on the deck. It was heaven. A little later I took Alexander to the pool. He'd never been swimming and he loved it. We had the whole Olympic-size pool to ourselves. What better way to learn to swim?

There still wasn't much open outside the Lemondrop, but that didn't matter. We ran and chased around the whole house playing. All the levels and balconies were perfect for play. I took the Skipper to the woods behind the house and taught him how to chop wood and how to whittle— things that were commonplace to me growing up, but magical to a kid growing up in New York City. He learned how to make a fire in the fireplace, and we all made s'mores. Arden and I talked and cooked and she raved about the house and how we'd set it up. Right now, I'm sitting on that deck writing. Sitting here writing I feel, more than just about anywhere else, that I'm who I'm supposed to be. It's my special place, even now. Three years later, with multiple Vermont trips under his belt, Alexander says the Yellow House is his favorite place. It's a beautiful thing when the people you love, love something you've created.

Alexander is doing swimmingly now, but back then, he was having a hard time at school. School was hard for me because I couldn't read, but I can only imagine how hard it was for him not understanding what people were saying. It must have been so terrifying for him. Alexander had a wonderful support team, but that was a hard year for him. He kept bringing home really dark pictures; people's eyes Xed out and blood and monsters.

It would break your heart. But, after our trip, he also brought home drawings of a little yellow house with flowers, rainbows, and smiling people. If we never made a penny on the Lemondrop, that would have made the whole endeavor worth it.

31

Fall

July turned to August and August fell into September. We'd filled the Lemondrop with travelers seeking a respite from the summer heat in the crisp Green Mountains. Now those mountains were bursting into a blaze of autumn colors. Things looked good for the Lemondrop. Things were looking up for the world as well. While still within the grip of Covid, a burgeoning feeling of hope crept into the world. We'd survived the spike in cases and deaths brought on by a new variant over the summer. The infections were on the decline and the vaccination rates on the rise. The world was starting to open up.

The Metropolitan Opera announced that they would be doing a partial season this year. I would be going back to work. Returning to the opera filled me with a mix of complicated feelings. A large part of me wished that I would have been able to establish a new life. A larger part of me, however, was incredibly proud of what I had accomplished during the pandemic and even more relieved to be able to go back to work at the opera. I still wanted a transition in my life, but I wasn't ready yet. I'd made great leaps and strides toward that goal— maybe the biggest of which was a sense of confidence. I'd always thought I could start a new business and make a huge life change, but the chasm between thinking it and doing it seemed too large to traverse. Now I knew I could do it. If that sense of confidence were the only thing I'd gained from the Lemondrop, that would have been monumental.

Hey, if I could make a go of a hospitality business in the middle of a global pandemic, what wasn't possible? I would be going back to the Met with a new appreciation for the job, with a lot of the petty daily grind issues washed away, and with the knowledge that it was, for me, temporary. Xanthus would be going back to work as well. His job at his old restaurant had evaporated, but when you have as much New York City fine dining experience as he, and a list of top chefs and restaurateurs as long as a Friday night waitlist, it's not hard to find work. He also longed for a new life. Like me, I think he felt much closer to that becoming a reality while at the same time relieved to go back to some normalcy as the world rebuilt.

We'd been so lucky in so many ways, not the least of which was the chance to make all of our mistakes and climb our way up the learning curve while not having to work another job, but not depending on the Lemondrop for our livelihood. Well, we haven't made all of our mistakes. Mistakes are perennial; they bloom eternal.

As I mentioned we'd filled up June, July, and August, and were doing well with September. And why not? New England in the fall... I mean come on, who wouldn't want a weekend escape into the Green Mountains as they ignite into a blaze of color? Then abruptly, it all stopped.

One week turned into two, and I began to wonder. It was our first October, maybe that was the mirror to mud season in the spring. A kind of lull between fall foliage and winter skiing. But that didn't make sense. October is still beautiful, and there's still lots to do. Besides, restaurants and shopping weren't shutting down like in the spring. Why weren't we getting any bookings? I kept looking at our listings. They looked good, but our views were down. Way down. Why?

I went to the internet. I scoured articles, browsed YouTube videos, and perused social media posts. The problem seemed to be isolated to just us. We'd been way ahead of the curve with bookings, but now we had fallen below the national and area averages. Then I found something. Something to try, at least.

I had been checking our listings from my laptop or my iPad. Not only had I been checking them from my devices, but I was also checking them from my account. If you know anything about the internet, you'll know companies love cookies as much as my niece. I was not getting an accurate picture of our listing. When I would search, even when I'd search without signing into my account, my devices were still filled with all the cookies from all the time I'd spent on Airbnb and Vrbo. Because I'd spent so much time looking at the Lemondrop in the past, surely that's what I wanted to see now. So that's what the algorithm showed me. One article suggested that you download a brand-new browser. Use that browser to do your searches, but don't ever sign in, and don't *ever* click on your listing. That way, you can do searches without tainting the results with past search data. And sure enough, there it was. On Airbnb, we were ranking in the hundreds. Weekend stays, week stays, stays with kids, stays with pets, all in the one hundreds, or two hundreds, or even three hundreds. Like I told you way back at the beginning if your listing doesn't at the very least rank in the top fifty, you might as well not be on the platform.

We'd been ranking consistently high. Our search results and bookings proved that, but something had changed in the last month. Here's something I can't stress enough–Airbnb and Vrbo will roll out large changes with fanfare, but they're also going to be constantly making small changes to their platforms, most of which they're not going to tell you about. I spent several hours going through every detail of our listing and found a score of little changes and additions to make. Next, I dove into our pricing. When we first started, I'd done extensive research on the pricing for our area. I'd set a weekend and weekday price for peak season and a weekend and weekday price for off-season. I adjusted for holidays, and I ran discounts when bookings were slow. All of that was great, but it wasn't enough.

Pricing, like most aspects of short-term rentals, is not set it and forget it. Pricing is also one of the major factors that determines your ranking in search results. Sure, Airbnb wants you to get as much as you can because their take is higher, but even more than that, they just want people to book. They don't have your mortgage or your overhead to worry about. They want people to book, and if a lower price gets that booking, so be it. I now have a protocol I do each morning (yup, every single morning). It includes a quick run through our listing on our account, a check of our ranking with various key search criteria on a clean browser, a quick analysis of the pricing in our area, and a tweaking of our own prices if need be. I've gotten this down to about fifteen minutes. I do it in the morning while I drink my coffee. It also helps me keep my finger on the pulse of the area and gives me a peek at what other short-term rental owners are doing. We had some of the same problems with our Vrbo, listing with one rather large difference. Our listing had been changed from a three-bedroom, three-bathroom, house to a zero-bedroom eight-bathroom house. Yup, who wants no bedrooms and eight bathrooms? Nobody. Who has no bedrooms and eight bathrooms? Maybe the porta potty zone of a construction site.

Our listing looked fine on our account, but when I searched on a clean browser, that's what I got. Despite being older, Vrbo's platform can be very glitchy. You have to keep an extra eye on your Vrbo listing. It took me two days and about six hours on the phone with customer service before I was able to get our listing fixed. Most of that time consisted of conversations like this:

Me: "Our listing says we don't have any bedrooms, and we have eight bathrooms."

Customer service: "Yes."

Me: "Well, we have three bedrooms and three bathrooms."

Customer service: "You should change that."

Me: "Yes, that's what I'm trying to do."

Customer service: "Change it in your listing."

Me: "Yes, I've tried that. In my listing, it shows up as correct."

Customer service: "Okay if it's correct, does that solve the issue?"

Me: "No, it's not correct in search results. Only on my listing."

Customer service: "Oh, you should change that then..."

Six hours of this sort of thing. We do get a lot of bookings through Vrbo but they can be a challenge.

It took me about a week, but I got our listings back up in the top twenty for most search results. Our views rocketed up, and our bookings quickly followed.

32

We Made It Through Our First Year

I promised you a year at the Lemondrop, but I'm gonna give you a little bit more. That is, after all one of our prime directives: exceed expectations. Although, now that I think of it, when did our first year at the Lemondrop begin? Did it start on November 6th, 2020, when we closed on the house? Maybe in August of 2020, when Xanthus, Paula, and I first drove up to West Dover and saw our little yellow house? Maybe it started forty years ago when a little boy in Kansas took his mother's peppermints and sold them door to door trying to start a business. Regardless of when our first year started, I know where I'd like to leave you on our journey, my dear reader. I've given it a lot of thought and there's a pretty clear moment when so many things in the world were changing and we, along with the world, were moving into a new era.

Mount Snow opened two weeks late in 2021. Not due to Covid this time. Covid was quickly coming under control. No, this time, it was good old-fashioned global warming. There was no snow and it was just too hot to make man-made snow for the slopes until the middle of December.

I was frustrated at first, but it didn't hurt our bookings much. We were pretty much at full occupancy all December through the first of the year. Remember Claudia? Well, our ice fall not only didn't faze her, she booked two months starting the first week in January. Along with Claudia, a couple of other return guests, and some newbies we were fully booked until the end of March. What we did have was a dead week between January 1st and January 6th, 2021.

We decided to use this as an opportunity for the whole family to experience the Lemondrop together. We'd had the house for more than a year, and yet never all been up there together. That's one of the tradeoffs for having a successful short-term rental. You're not going to get to spend a lot of time there yourself. Anemone, Francisco and the two kids went up first and had a night together alone in the Lemondrop. Paula, Xanthus, and I (and of course Poppy) drove up the next morning.

The house felt full and alive with all six of us cooking and laughing, playing games and talking. For me, it was a beautiful thing to see my family together enjoying our new house, enjoying our new business. As a family, life had thrown us many challenges, at times splintering us away from each other.

This past year of global shutdown coupled with starting a new business had both brought us closer together and strained our relationships. As I sat in the comfy burgundy chair and watched everyone bustling about, I couldn't help but marvel at how each of them, each of us, had grown.

I marveled at my brother's meticulous attention to detail, his profound commitment to service, and the enjoyment of others. He wants everything to be perfect for our guests. He wants them to be wowed when they arrive and want for nothing during their stay. What's maybe even more impressive to me is the way he tries to anticipate our guests' needs and solve them before those needs ever arise. It's a thankless job to anticipate problems before they arise, to pamper people in a way that they don't realize they're being pampered. It's a beautiful thing.

I watched Francisco, a man I was only beginning to know, play with his children. I was jealous of his zest for life his curiosity, and the way he let it inform his intelligence. I was blown away by his journey so far in life from the mountains in Colombia to Spain, to the United States. He'd risen from a little boy in a strange land to a man quickly rising in his field. A man with a beautiful family.

My sister. I've always been so proud of my sister. She moved up to New York City straight out of high school to be a performer. The courage and dedication that requires would be more than enough to earn anyone's respect. But it didn't stop there. After a few years in New York, she decided that she didn't want theater to be her life. That's a very hard decision. I've seen so many performers continue to try years after they've lost the love for the stage. Without that love, theater is a brutal life. She worked three jobs and put herself through college all the while rising in the banking industry to where she is now, a regional manager of one of the country's most respected banks. She wanted a family and she made it happen, complete with two astounding children and an honest to goodness white picket fence. With her drive and determination, how could Lemondrop fail?

And Paula, my mother. I could absolutely not have done this without her. When we'd started, we gave her a stake in the business in exchange for the use of her car and her name on our listing. We wanted her to be involved and to have a kind of hobby outside of her grandkids. Her participation and value to the business has exceeded my wildest expectations. She has been my partner on this journey in the truest sense of the word. Let Paula be a lesson to anyone who thinks it's too late. At seventy, she sold her home in Kansas and moved across the country to start a whole new life to take care of her grandkids. At seventy-three, she started a business, fell in love with a brand-new state, and became an expert in a field she'd never even known existed. Yes, the next time you think it's too late to try something new, think about Paula.

I watched these people whom I love so much running around the house I've come to love so much, and my thoughts turned to myself. I'd grown over this last year, year and a half. My brain had always been brimming with business ideas, most of which never made the jump from my brain to the world. The ones that did obtained lukewarm success at best. The Lemondrop was different.

I wasn't cutting corners. I was doing it right, and the results were beyond my dreams. Well, that's not true. My dreams have always been large, but when I think how worried I was that we wouldn't be able to cover our mortgage, I think that was my expectation. I think when I started, I just hoped that the business wouldn't drag me (and my family) under financially. It was surreal dealing with deposits and revenue in the thousands. The Lemondrop was unquestionably a success. We'd been covering our bills since our second week of business. We'd earned enough to pay me back the money I'd loaned the business. We'd been taking big, bear-size bites out of the credit card debt we'd accrued during start up. And, while I really can't take credit for this, we'd bought the Lemondrop a few weeks before the housing market soared. Houses listed in our area were selling for cash offers well above their asking price in less than twenty-four hours. Our house had appreciated more than 30 percent in the year since we'd bought it. And it wasn't just money.

I'd only had brief glimpses into our guests's experiences; the messages through the platforms, a social media post here and there, but I often thought of them. I think about the family vacations, the romantic getaways, the adventures we'd helped facilitate. I marveled at how many memories the Lemondrop must occupy and what those memories must mean to their owners. The Lemondrop Lodge has had a positive impact on the community, on our guests, and if it doesn't sound too grandiose, the Lemondrop, in its own little way, has had a positive impact on the world. The Lemondrop certainly has a positive effect on me. It gave me a confidence and ease in the world I didn't realize I lacked. Remember Arden? The Lemondrop wasn't my only pandemic birthed business. She and I had invented a product, prototyped it, tested it, manufactured it, and brought it to market. As I'm writing this, the Read To Me Recordable Book Buddy is available not only directly to consumers on our website GiveReadToMe.com. It's also available in eighty-eight independent bookstores in forty-seven states and three countries. I don't think I would have had the gumption to start Read To Me if I hadn't had the early success with the Lemondrop.

Wednesday morning, everyone was scurrying about preparing the Lemondrop for our next guests and packing our things. Someone had turned on the TV. It wasn't me. I rarely turn on the TV at the Lemondrop. Why disturb the peace outside world?

We were all bustling about. It's funny; you would think that more people cleaning and doing a turnover would make it go quicker, but oftentimes they just get in each other's way. We had a guest coming in the next day, so we had to get the place all spiffed up after our stay. Something was happening on the news. I kept seeing glimpses of the Capitol Building and an angry crowd. I was focused on cleaning, so I didn't have much idea what was going on. We all continued bustling about, and I started to glean that there was an angry mob at the US Capitol

Building in Washington, DC, where the 2020 presidential election results were being certified. Were they going to storm the Capitol? The last couple of years were surreal. More than once, I thought about how the Lemondrop could be our escape if the world started imploding— plague, nuclear war, civil war, natural disasters. Up on a mountain in Vermont wouldn't be a bad place to hunker down as the world sorted itself out. I was grateful that we were all here together.

I continued to clean because we had a guest coming and that's what you do. I kept nervously glancing at the TV, afraid each time that I'd see people storming the Capitol. I was afraid I'd see people being shot and mowed down by the Secret Service. Would that spark a civil war? On that day, it seemed very possible. At some point, I noticed my little niece. She and my nephew were being very good, keeping out of the way while we all got the Lemondrop ready. My nephew was playing foosball, but my niece was confused. She didn't understand what was happening. The two of us went up to the master bedroom, sat on the bed, and I tried to explain. Why were people so angry? What was going on? She's a very smart cookie, but the world is a hard thing to understand. I'm a smart cookie, but the world is a hard thing to explain. As I'd mentioned before, I'm not a kid kinda guy. I have found, though talking to my niece and nephew and Alexander that there is nothing like a conversation with a child to really show you what you understand about a given topic and what you don't. They are going to have questions and they are going to want answers. It's a beautiful thing the way they force you to stretch your mind. Children also don't have all the conditioning and years of thought routines that those of us more advanced in years have. I've found when talking with my niece that I often learn just as much as she does. She and I didn't learn to understand the world that morning, but sitting there in our house, talking with her, with the rest of my family working together to get the place ready, I felt a burgeoning hope. The world was moving to a new phase. It seemed that the virus' grasp on us all was waning, and as I sat there on the bed talking with my niece, I began to think, or at least hope, that the violence at the Capitol was the death throes of our division as a nation.

Whatever was going on with the outside world, the Lemondrop was also moving into a new stage. Each member of my family had learned and grown so much. Somewhere along the line, I'd transformed from a novice to something of an expert. The Lemondrop was profitable and running smoothly. Our guests were happy and our calendar was full. What had seemed like such a hair-brained idea— starting a short-term rental business in the middle of a global pandemic— had miraculously worked.

The first year at the Lemondrop was a wild adventure. There is more to learn. There are more challenges ahead, but they fill me with excitement. Even now writing this, I'm giddy thinking of what the future might hold and of our continuing adventure at the Lemondrop Lodge.

The end

Or is it...

ACKNOWLEDGMENTS

There are a great many people without whom this book, and indeed this whole adventure, would have never been possible.

First off, all our lovely guests. Thank you for trusting us with your most valuable asset— your time. We are honored you chose to spend it with us. The state and people of Vermont. What more can I say? You are beautiful. All of the local businesses and people of West Dover. It's because of you that our little community is such a magical destination.

My family. Each of you brought your own unique talents without any of which the Lemondop would not be what it is today. And, of course, my mother— Paula. I want to thank her for writing a chapter for this book. I want to thank her for being there whenever I needed help or just a sounding board on this adventure. I want to thank her for helping to make me the man I am today.

HAVE A LOOK

Would you like some visuals to go along with the story? Maybe you just want to see our adventure continue. Follow us on social media.

Instagram ~ YouTube ~ Facebook ~ TikTok

@lemondroplodge

HAVE A LOOK

LEMONDROP SERVICES

Lemondr p
Short Term Rental Services

LEMONDROP SERVICES

Elevate Your Short-Term Rental with Lemondrop Services

Embark on your Short-Term Rental (STR) venture with a trusted ally by your side – Lemondrop Short-Term Rental Services. We're not just service providers; we're your seasoned co-navigators in the STR universe.

Why Choose Lemondrop?

Expertise Born from Experience: You've read about our first year, and since then we've navigated the STR landscape, gathering invaluable insights and strategies. We're eager to pass on this knowledge to you, our fellow STR enthusiasts.

Boost Your Listing's Visibility: In the crowded world of STR, standing out is key. We specialize in catapulting your listing to the forefront, ensuring it catches the eye of your ideal guests.

Maximize Guest Experience: We believe that a memorable guest experience translates to repeat visits and glowing reviews. Our tools and tactics are designed to elevate your guests' stay, making your property their preferred choice.

Resources at Your Fingertips: For the DIY aficionados, we offer a rich collection of eBooks and digital downloads, packed with actionable tips and strategies.

Personalized Consulting: If you prefer a more guided approach, our personalized consulting services are tailored to meet your unique needs. Whether it's refining your property's appeal or navigating guest relations, we're here to assist.

For Hosts of All Stripes: It doesn't matter if you're just stepping into the world of STR or you're a seasoned host looking to refine your approach – Lemondrop has the tools, knowledge, and support you need to thrive.

Your Success is Our Mission: At Lemondrop, we measure our success by yours. Our goal is to empower you with the knowledge, strategies, and tools to turn your investment into a flourishing STR venture.

Join the Lemondrop Community Today

Elevate your STR journey. Contact us to discover how we can help you transform your short-term rental venture into a resounding success. With Lemondrop, you're not just managing a rental; you're creating exceptional experiences and lasting memories.

Visit us at:

Lemondropservices.com

www.ingramcontent.com/pod-product-compliance
Lightning Source LLC
LaVergne TN
LVHW041758060526
838201LV00046B/1037